THE RELATIONSHIP RESCUE WORKBOOK

THE *R*ELATIONSHIP
RESCUE WORKBOOK

Exercises and Self-Tests

to Help You Reconnect

with Your Partner

PHILLIP C. McGRAW, PH.D.

HYPERION

NEW YORK

ISBN: 0-7868-8604-8

FIRST EDITION

10   9   8   7   6   5   4   3   2

contents

PART I: RECOVER YOUR CORE
Based on the Prologue and Chapter 1 of Relationship Rescue:
A Seven-Step Strategy for Reconnecting with Your Partner

PART II: UNCOVER THE TROUBLE
Based on Chapters 2 through 4 of Relationship Rescue:
A Seven-Step Strategy for Reconnecting with Your Partner

about this workbook

We all have room to improve the quality of our lives in general and our relationships in particular. If you have read or are reading *Relationship Rescue: A Seven-Step Strategy for Reconnecting with Your Partner*, you know that any change or improvement has to start with you. The truth is, this is not a burden—it is an opportunity, because it means that you are in control. Be glad that change, either personal or relational, starts with you, because you are the only person over whom you have control. Any impact on your partner and your relationship will follow the impact you have on yourself. For now, focus on you. You have in your hands a worthy tool for a worthy desire. But it is only a tool. It will not change you or your life. Only you can do that. You have within you everything you need to make a new, better life for yourself and, subsequently, for your partner.

In this workbook and the book it accompanies, I have set out a clear-eyed, realistic, and effective blueprint for getting real about your relationship with you and your relationship with your partner and for putting both back on track. The two books are designed to be companions. The hardcover book offers you the information and tools you will need to understand what's wrong in your relationship and begin the process of restoring it. The workbook gives you a totally private place to complete a wide variety of exercises that are crucial to the process. Some of these exercises appear in the hardcover book, but many do not. In the interest of confidentiality, I encourage you to place all your written responses in the privacy of your own workbook.

Read the books and do the work, and you will reclaim the power to shape the life you live. You will rediscover the strength of character residing within you, no matter how many layers of denial, distortion, and life experience have covered it up. By getting back in touch with who you are, you will launch a lifelong process of reconnection with your relationship partner that will transform the life you have been living.

All you need to get started is the commitment to stick with it, no matter what. Life can be a hell of a lot of work, but what else have you got to do? You need the determination to require more of yourself in every area of your life. You are about to give yourself and your partner the greatest gift you can: a heart and mind in tune with your inner values and potential for greatness.

You will not find perfection. You will not change your partner. Instead, and much more to the point, you will reconnect with your own best self. When you do, you will become a person who inspires everyone around you to rise to a new, nobler level. You will live in such a way that others will know that you refuse to settle for anything less than an honest, active, and abiding love.

part i

RECOVER YOUR CORE

Before you begin this portion of the *Relationship Rescue Workbook*, read or reread the Prologue and Chapter 1 of *Relationship Rescue: A Seven-Step Strategy for Reconnecting with Your Partner*.

GET REAL — RECONNECTING WITH
YOUR CORE

Your relationship is in trouble, and you want to fix it. Or your relationship is good, and you want to preserve or stabilize it. But to do so, you will have to be willing to put first things first, and start the fixing where the work needs to begin: not with the relationship, and not with your partner, but with yourself. The person you are in your relationship will make the most important and life-changing difference possible. So who have you been in this relationship in the past that allowed it to be or contributed to it being in so much trouble? Who are you deep inside? What is strong, good, and excellent within you? And what's keeping the best that is in you from making its way into your relationship? It's time to find out. As you work through the exercises in this section, reach within yourself to discover—or rediscover—your "core of consciousness." There is a self, an identity, that may well have gotten buried over the years. As we reflect back on how you have come to this point in your life, you will be refreshed as you revisit those truths, values, and beliefs that were at one time so very, very clear. It will be from this core of values, talents, instincts, and strengths that all the other work you do will flow.

THE BEST PEOPLE

In a busy, stressful life, it's easy enough to lose track of what you admire and aspire to be as a human being. You can reconnect with some of the qualities that mean the most to you by taking stock of what you esteem in others. We all need targets and goals to strive for. Emulating those whom we admire is a positive thing. It is not an attempt to be someone you are not; it is simply choosing to incorporate into your being that which you admire in others. To help you focus on qualities worthy of incorporation, identify the three people that you admire the most, and write their names in the spaces that follow. They may be family members, friends, or famous people—whoever exhibits the qualities you consider most important in a person. After you have selected your three people, list at least five qualities that describe what you most admire about them.

1.

   a.

   b.

c.

d.

e.

2.

a.

b.

c.

d.

e.

3.

a.

b.

c.

d.

e.

When you were born, you came equipped with your own set of excellent qualities that acted as your internal compass for living effectively. At some point, you probably had a strong sense of some or all of these qualities. But over time, you experienced defeats, disappointments, and disillusionments that have sent your best self fleeing for cover. These characteristics are not lost; they are just buried under the crap that sometimes defines life. Hope and optimism give way to cynicism and resignation. You cannot operate from this distorted base of experience. Your goal is to uncover that which at one time defined you with clarity and power. Right now, I want you to call those qualities out of hiding. The people you just identified and the descriptions you made of each should help you take a new look at yourself. Which of the characteristics you most admire in others exist in you, even if they're hidden? List them in the chart that follows under "In a Perfect World." What other qualities could you add that are important to you? List them, too. Include physical, professional, spiritual, emotional, relational, financial, and intellectual qualities.

In a Perfect World, I Am . . .	In Reality, I Am . . .
Physically	
Professionally	
Spiritually	
Emotionally	
Relationally	
Financially	
Intellectually	

IN REALITY,
WHAT ARE
YOU DOING?

Now finish the chart. Briefly describe how the reality of your life differs from the ideal or potential regarding these qualities. You have to get real and be as honest as you possibly can. Until you face where you've gone off-center, you can't work your way back. Until you name what you want, you can't claim it for yourself. When I say get real, I mean that you have to get no-kidding, drop-dead, unvarnished honest with yourself about who you have become. If you have started to live in a gutless, don't-make-waves fashion, then say so. If you have become embittered and hostile, then be willing to admit that. Remember, you can't change what you do not acknowledge, so don't cheat yourself with some kind of gloss-over con job at this critical stage.

NEGATIVE
VOICES

One of the battering rams that helped break down your core of consciousness was the negative input you received from others. These negative voices can be ever-present and create tremendous doubt at critical times in your life. You need to identify the negative attitudes you have about yourself that helped program you for failure in your relationship. Read the following statements. Put a check mark beside every statement that describes a negative message you've received (and perhaps believed) from others about yourself. Again, be totally honest.

1. I'm lazy.
2. I talk too much (not enough).
3. I don't know how the world really works.
4. I'm too fat (thin).
5. I think of no one but myself.
6. I'm a know-it-all.
7. I'm stupid.
8. I complain too much.
9. I'm never satisfied.
10. I don't pay attention.
11. I don't think ahead.
12. I have no opinions of my own.

13. I never listen.
14. I'm ugly.
15. I'm messy.
16. I have no taste.
17. I'm too ambitious (not ambitious enough).
18. I am just like my father (mother).
19. I never practice what I preach.
20. I always (never) want sex.
21. I assume the worst.
22. I'm a nag.
23. I never accept the blame (always blame someone else).
24. I neglect my responsibilities.
25. I have a chip on my shoulder.

Now add ten more negative thoughts that uniquely define you. These should be thoughts that were not on the list of twenty-five given here, but that nevertheless program you for failure. List them in the same short, precise language as the first twenty-five.

For every statement that you checked, as well as for the ten that you listed, identify the source of that message in your life. It may be your partner, a family member, a teacher, a preacher, the media, your parents, your neighbor, or your boss. It certainly may be you and your own self-critical analysis, which is ever-present. Don't accept that you don't know or remember where you heard a negative message. Such messages come from somewhere. Only when you identify the source can you begin to rise above the message.

WHAT DO YOU THINK ALL DAY?

The negative messages you receive from others have tremendous power to shape your view of yourself and the way you live. You may have heard those messages long in the past, or you may hear them for moments every day. But their power can't compare to the power of what you tell yourself about yourself. Your own "negative tapes" travel with you twenty-four hours a day, seven days a week.

Right now, get in touch with what you say to yourself about you. I want you to write for five minutes without stopping. (You will need to use a separate piece of paper.) Use the ten negative messages you listed in the previous exercise to start this internal dialogue. Expand upon them, add to them—but write nonstop and as quickly as possible. Set a timer before you start so that you won't waste time or thought on how long you've been writing. Just write whatever comes into your mind: Include aspects of self-image, self-esteem, and self-worth; satisfaction in your performance; security in your relationships; comfort with your place in the world. Don't worry about grammar, spelling, or writing whole sentences. If the timer goes off and you have more on your mind, keep writing until the flow stops on its own. If you run out of things to say, keep writing whatever pops into your mind for the full five minutes.

Now go back and read what you've written. Underline every negative statement about yourself. Look for judgments, self-criticisms, excuses, and justifications for letting yourself down. These are the messages that scab over your core of consciousness and keep you from living with excellence.

THE HAPPIEST TIME OF MY LIFE

In writing, describe the time in your life when you were the happiest you've ever been. As you write, answer these questions *in as much detail as you can remember*. When was it? Where were you? Who were you with? What were you doing? Why were you doing it? How were you doing it? How did you feel? How did you look? How did you perceive your surroundings? Let your imagination and emotions run free here. One of our greatest gifts from God is the ability to travel in time and recapture the feelings and thoughts that defined an earlier period. Be very specific, and write this as though you were describing a scene for a movie or a play.

A PERSONAL VISION

You've just concluded some self-examination that I hope has begun to reconnect you to your core of consciousness, to get you focused back on the uniqueness of who you were (and still are) before life started kicking your butt. At the same time, you've begun to identify specific ways in which you've lost touch with that set of values and qualities. Analysis such as this is vital, but it isn't enough. You need to give it time and attention, as well, to get the result you're hoping for.

I'm talking right now about what you want for *you*. We'll get into what you want for your relationship as we move forward. For the moment, concentrate on yourself, because who you are plays a critical role in what kind of relationship you have. You must guard against feeling selfish here for focusing so much attention on yourself. While it may be politically correct to put on your martyr hat with the "I'll be fine" attitude, that does nothing less than cheat you and everyone who loves you and depends on you. You must take care of yourself before you can take care of others, and this is the time to do that.

First, review everything you've done so far. This is very important—don't hurry through the review. When you've looked everything over carefully, write a description of yourself as you want to be. Write it in the way that you would introduce someone else whom you love and admire. Remember: This isn't fairy tale time; this is *you* as you *want to be*.

ACT ON IT! Before we move on, I'm going to ask you to do one more thing. This is an action assignment that will help you experience your power to choose differently in the future from what you've chosen in the past. Read over your "personal vision" above, and circle each positive characteristic you've described. Copy them below as a list. Then choose just one. For the next week, "act" that characteristic at every appropriate opportunity. Notice yourself doing it, and keep track of every instance in the space below. Describe how you feel every time you exercise the quality, and describe what happens around you. Be sure to notice and record how others respond to you as you actively put this positive quality into play. I want you to learn how to behave your way to success. This is not a "fake-it-till-you-make-it" philosophy. Instead, it is a "create-your-own-experience" approach to living. Act out this characteristic with zeal and passion, and be patient. You will get better at it as you move along.

chapter 1

IT'S YOUR TIME; IT'S YOUR TURN

Y ou've taken some time to reconnect with yourself. You've also given some fresh thought to the values and qualities that make you as capable as anyone to love your life and build a positive, healthy relationship. But your present experience doesn't come close to what you want—or what you can have—with work and a solid strategy. Now I want you to get real about your own responsibility for the mess your relationship has become. Take this opportunity to pull away the layers of denial that have allowed you to actively, consistently, and efficiently live in and support a bad relationship. This is the necessary first step that will allow you to stop sabotaging yourself and your relationship.

DR. PHIL'S RELATIONSHIP STRESS TEST (given to participants on *The Oprah Winfrey Show*)

Just in case you're looking at the hard work it takes to get a bad relationship on good footing, and you're tempted to think, "Hey, we're not so bad," it's time to face what's happening to you as a result of keeping your relationship as it is. This stress test will give you a sense of the life-damaging stress that your bad relationship produces in you. Unchallenged stress is a proven, extreme danger to your health and happiness. And a bad intimate relationship is one of the prime sources of such stress. So check it out and see how you score. This is a common-sense behavioral inventory rather than a standardized test. Give broad interpretations to the questions, and be brutally honest in your answers.

1. Do you or your partner hold a grudge after an argument? **Yes** **No**
2. Do you or your partner frequently keep your feelings bottled up? **Yes** **No**
3. Do discussions often turn into heated arguments? **Yes** **No**
4. In an argument, are there often personal attacks, such as name calling? **Yes** **No**
5. Do you and your partner treat your relationship like a competition? For example, do you fight to be right? **Yes** **No**
6. Have you stopped looking forward to spending time with your partner? **Yes** **No**
7. Do you withhold affection from your partner? **Yes** **No**
8. Do you or your partner avoid talking about serious issues? **Yes** **No**
9. Have you given up on trying to meet your relationship needs with your partner? **Yes** **No**
10. Are you filling the emotional void left by your relationship with other people and activities? **Yes** **No**
11. Do your arguments end with one or both of you feeling worse? **Yes** **No**
12. Do you or your partner feel "on guard" when you're together? **Yes** **No**
13. Do you often feel trapped in your relationship? **Yes** **No**
14. Do you feel your mate doesn't understand you? **Yes** **No**
15. Do you often feel angry or frustrated with your partner? **Yes** **No**
16. Do you feel your mate does not appreciate you? **Yes** **No**
17. Do you often feel lonely in your relationship? **Yes** **No**
18. Do you feel powerless to change the relationship? **Yes** **No**

19. Do you feel pessimistic or negative about your future?   **Yes**   **No**

20. Do you feel like your best is never good enough for your partner?   **Yes**   **No**

Total Number of Questions Answered Yes _____

Scoring

0 to 4	Good relationship, rare stress
5 to 10	Relationship needs work, occasional exposure to stress
11 to 15	Seriously troubled, under frequent stress
16 to 20	Relationship is damaging, extremely stressful

Again, this is not a standardized test found in a textbook somewhere, but it does raise a number of typical stress-producing issues. If you scored over 10, you are in a stressful relationship that needs to change.

WHAT'S YOUR PART?

I've said it before, and I'll say it again: You are not a victim! You are the one who created your current life. You sure had some help, but that doesn't let you off the hook. (Understand that I am talking about your *current* life and circumstances. If you were abused, molested, or neglected as a child, that absolutely was not your fault. If these were your circumstances, they were tragic, and I am sorry that they occurred. But you are making the choices *now*. Be clear about this so you don't allow yourself to feel sorry for yourself or think that I don't understand the tragedies of your earlier life.) Take a moment right now to identify the aspects of your current relationship that bother you the most. Then we'll see what part you play in the here and now and in your adult history. Finish each of the following phrases with five different endings that pertain to your relationship.

I see red when . . . (*anger*)

1.

2.

3.

4.

5.

I want to pull my hair out when . . . (*frustration*)

1.

2.

3.

4.

5.

I want to run away from home when . . . (*denial*)

1.

2.

3.

4.

5.

I want to call the guys in the white coats when . . . (*accusation*)

1.

2.

3.

4.

5.

Looking at the sentences you produced above, I want you to identify what feel like the *five worst* qualities or traits of your relationship right now and list them here.

1.

2.

3.

4.

5.

Now write a paragraph that finishes the following phrase. Give this plenty of time. You'll have reason to refer to this later.

The reasons I have allowed these aspects of my relationship to continue unchanged are . . .

If you were honest with yourself, you just made a catalog of your excuses, rationalizations, and self-justifications. Keep these in mind, because these have got to go!

WHAT'S THE
PAYOFF?

There's only one reason why you haven't changed the bad stuff in your relationship: You're getting something out of it. I'm not saying that you're getting something healthy or positive, but people do not continue in situations, attitudes, or actions that do not give them a payoff. That's true of everyone—including you. So what's your payoff for continuing with the "five worst" aspects that you just identified above? I've offered a list of twenty-five possibilities. Put a check mark beside every item that rings true.

I allow this (any negative aspect) to continue because when I do . . .

_____ I look good in comparison to my partner
_____ I don't have to put in a lot of effort
_____ I get more sympathy
_____ I can avoid looking too closely at myself
_____ It gives me more freedom
_____ It gives me an excuse for not trying harder
_____ I can demand what I want because my partner feels guilty
_____ I can't fail if I don't try
_____ I don't have to make some tough choices
_____ It makes me feel like a saint

_____ Other people want to help me
_____ I can avoid fights
_____ My partner leaves me alone
_____ I have an excuse for spending more time away from home
_____ I have an excuse for being unfaithful
_____ I can blame my partner for not having a better life myself
_____ I secretly enjoy the drama
_____ I believe it makes me more interesting to others
_____ This way, I can keep my vulnerable parts hidden
_____ I get attention this way, even though it's negative
_____ It serves my partner right
_____ I'm afraid of being alone
_____ It's easier than fixing it
_____ It's safer than facing it
_____ It gives me the upper hand
_____ It hides my own faults

These are just examples of the payoffs that keep people in bad situations. Look back over your list of negatives and identify at least one payoff for each (use the list or discover your own payoff) that helps keep you in your situation.

A SELF-
ANALYSIS

Look at the first item on your "five worst" list. I want you to recall a particular incident between you and your partner that illustrates the negative aspect, quality, or trait you've identified. Write a paragraph in the space here to describe this quality or trait in action.

Now answer the following questions as honestly and thoroughly as you can. This is not an exercise designed to make you feel worse about yourself or your relationship. The more you identify and understand your own responsibility for your relationship problems, the more ready you'll be to make the necessary changes. Let me warn you: The following questions take real courage to answer honestly. Before you get defensive and retreat into denial, make no mistake about the following: Whatever your life and relationships include, *you set it up that way*. That does not mean that you did it on purpose. Nonetheless, it means you are the responsible party in your current life. Answer these questions from that point of view, and you will maximize this exercise.

1. How did *you* set up this aspect of your relationship?

2. How have *you* permitted it to exist?

3. How do *you* participate in continuing it?

4. What do *you* do that makes it worse?

Repeat this exercise with each of the traits you identified.

Describe an incident illustrating the second negative aspect, quality, or trait.

1. How did *you* set up this aspect of your relationship?

2. How have *you* permitted it to exist?

3. How do *you* participate in continuing it?

4. What do *you* do that makes it worse?

Describe an incident illustrating the third negative aspect, quality, or trait.

1. How did *you* set up this aspect of your relationship?

2. How have *you* permitted it to exist?

3. How do *you* participate in continuing it?

4. What do *you* do that makes it worse?

Describe an incident illustrating the fourth negative aspect, quality, or trait.

1. How did *you* set up this aspect of your relationship?

2. How have *you* permitted it to exist?

3. How do *you* participate in continuing it?

4. What do *you* do that makes it worse?

Describe an incident illustrating the fifth negative aspect, quality, or trait.

1. How did *you* set up this aspect of your relationship?

2. How have *you* permitted it to exist?

3. How do *you* participate in continuing it?

4. What do *you* do that makes it worse?

YOUR BAG
OF TRICKS

Look over the five incidents and your analyses of them. From those written exercises, I want you to create a list here of how you sabotage yourself and your relationship in those examples. In other words, you need to identify specific attitudes and behaviors *in you* that are blocking your forward movement toward a better relationship. What do you think in the midst of the interaction? What do you say and do? How do you push your own buttons? What hidden agendas come into play, and what do you do after the immediate situation ends? Look for and list:

Thoughts

Spoken words

Actions

Reactions

Silent intentions

Subsequent behaviors

The attitudes and behaviors you have just uncovered from five particular incidents in your relationship are probably not unique to those incidents. They are attitudes and behaviors that have become integral ingredients in your relationship. You choose to think and act in these ways, even though they have destructive power that pulls your relationship apart. But you can choose to leave behind these destructive mindsets and habits. That's what rescuing your relationship is all about. You're learning to *know* better so you can *do* better.

TEST YOUR
READINESS

I want you to ask yourself the following questions and answer them *with complete honesty*. If you answer "no" to any of these questions, stop and take the time to figure out why you're still hanging on to this destructive mindset. Then describe specifically what it will take to change that "no" into a "yes."

Can you forget what you think you know about managing relationships?

Can you decide to measure the quality of your relationship based on results instead of intentions or promises?

Can you decide that you would rather be happy than right?

Can you stop playing the blame game and recognize that it is a new day?

Can you be willing to move your position on how you approach and engage your partner?

Can you be willing to get real and be honest with yourself, about yourself, no matter how painful it is?

Can you stop the denial and be completely, totally honest about the state of your current relationship?

Until you've honestly answered yes to every one of these questions, you're not ready to move on.

PROJECT
STATUS

Reread pages 17 through 19 in my book *Relationship Rescue*. Now write a paragraph describing what it will take to put your relationship on Project Status. Be very specific. Get into the *who*, *what*, *where*, *when*, *how*, and *why* of it. With this step, you can begin working to get what you want, to stop the pain, and to create more of what's best in a relationship.

part ii

Uncover the Trouble

Before you begin this portion of the *Relationship Rescue Workbook*, read or reread Chapters 2 through 4 of *Relationship Rescue.*

chapter 2

DEFINING THE PROBLEM

In Part I of this workbook, you concentrated on getting in touch and reconnecting with your core of consciousness—the strengths and values that need to be activated to let you make the life you want. You also began to understand that you are the one who put you where you are. You are responsible for the condition of your relationship. Now you need to take your understanding to a deeper level. You need to *diagnose* the trouble that has developed in your relationship. A list of examples may help you locate some of your problems—but it won't give you the depth of information and insight you need to make lifelong, positive changes in your relationship. As you enter this phase of relationship rescue, commit yourself again to total reality, complete honesty, and ruthless integrity. Don't settle for anything but the truth, the whole truth, and nothing but the truth.

Note to the reader: Much to my publisher's chagrin, I insisted on reproducing several of the tests in this section verbatim from the hardcover. At the risk of making the workbook too long, I have included these tests here so that they might be referred to and worked with under one cover. These are not tests or profiles to be taken once and then forgotten. Each one identifies strengths and weaknesses, and therefore needs to be constantly referenced in identifying resources and goals. I hope the convenience of having them here is worth the argument I had with the publisher.

PERSONAL
CONCEPTS
PROFILE

The following questionnaire will draw on your power of association. I've given you the start of forty-two questions. I want you to write down what comes to your mind quickly and easily. Don't overthink this. Your first instincts are likely to be your truest and most revealing.

1. I tend to deny _____

_____

_____

2. I am happiest when _____

_____

_____

3. Sometimes I _____

_____

_____

4. What makes me angry is _____

_____

_____

5. I wish _____

_____

_____

6. I hate it when _____

_____

_____

7. When I get angry I _____
_____
_____

8. I would give anything if my partner would _____
_____
_____

9. Sometimes _____
_____
_____

10. I would be more lovable if _____
_____
_____

11. My mother and father _____
_____
_____

12. If only I had _____
_____
_____

13. My best quality is _____
_____
_____

14. Sometimes at night _____
_____
_____

15. When I was a child _____
_____
_____

16. My worst trait is _____
_____
_____

17. My life really changed when _____
_____
_____

18. If my relationship ends it will be because _____
_____
_____

19. My partner hates it when I _____
_____
_____

20. When I am alone I _____
_____
_____

21. My partner gets angry when _____
_____
_____

22. My partner's greatest fear is _____
_____
_____

23. It hurts me when my partner _____
_____
_____

24. I feel the most lonely when _____
_____
_____

25. I am afraid _____

_____

_____

_____

26. I love _____

_____

_____

_____

27. We used to laugh more because _____

_____

_____

_____

28. It would be best if _____

_____

_____

_____

29. Friends _____

_____

_____

_____

30. I feel like a phony when _____

_____

_____

_____

31. I can't forgive _____

_____

_____

_____

32. Together we _____

_____

_____

33. What surprises me is _____

_____

_____

_____

34. I believe _____

_____

_____

35. Other people think _____

_____

_____

36. Men _____

_____

_____

37. Women _____

_____

_____

38. I regret _____

_____

_____

39. It doesn't pay to _____

_____

_____

40. It helps when we _____

_____

_____

41. If only _____

_____

_____

42. We never seem to _____

_____

_____

Based on your responses here, you're ready to evaluate what you've uncovered and answer the following five questions. Write at least two paragraphs for each, using the items listed in parentheses as your starting point.

What do these answers tell you about anger in your life and your relationship? (See items 4, 6, 7, 16, 17, 24, 25, 31.)

What do these answers tell you about fear in your life? (See items 1, 2, 14, 25, 27, 30.)

What do these answers tell you about the loneliness in your life and relationship? (See items 2, 8, 10, 14, 20, 23, 24, 42.)

What do these answers tell you about blame and forgiveness in your life and relationship? (See items 4, 6, 8, 11, 12, 16, 19, 31, 38, 41.)

What do these answers tell you about the dreams in your life and relationship? (See items 2, 3, 5, 8, 12, 26, 28, 34, 41, 42.)

RELATIONSHIP
HEALTH
PROFILE

Now let's move on to an overview of your relationship and find out about its overall health. Again, be honest, but answer without mulling. Your first reaction will tell you more than a response you have thought out.

1.	I am satisfied with my sex life.	**True**	**False**
2.	My partner doesn't really listen to me.	**True**	**False**
3.	I trust my partner.	**True**	**False**
4.	I feel picked on and put down.	**True**	**False**
5.	I am hopeful about our future.	**True**	**False**
6.	It is not easy to share my feelings.	**True**	**False**
7.	My partner often says, "I love you."	**True**	**False**
8.	Sometimes I feel rage.	**True**	**False**
9.	I feel appreciated.	**True**	**False**
10.	I am out of control.	**True**	**False**
11.	My partner is there for me in hard times.	**True**	**False**
12.	My partner is harsh in his or her criticism.	**True**	**False**
13.	My partner understands me.	**True**	**False**
14.	I fear my partner is bored.	**True**	**False**
15.	My partner doesn't like to share what's on his or her mind.	**True**	**False**
16.	I imagine myself divorced.	**True**	**False**
17.	My relationship is what I always dreamed of.	**True**	**False**
18.	I know I am right.	**True**	**False**
19.	My partner treats me with dignity and respect.	**True**	**False**
20.	My partner is a taker.	**True**	**False**

21.	We often do fun things together.	**True**	**False**
22.	Sometimes I just want to hurt my partner.	**True**	**False**
23.	I feel loved.	**True**	**False**
24.	I would rather lie than deal with a problem.	**True**	**False**
25.	We still have a lot of passion in our relationship.	**True**	**False**
26.	I am trapped with no escape.	**True**	**False**
27.	My partner thinks I am fun to be with.	**True**	**False**
28.	Our relationship has gotten boring.	**True**	**False**
29.	We enjoy going out on dates alone.	**True**	**False**
30.	My partner is ashamed of me.	**True**	**False**
31.	We trust each other a great deal.	**True**	**False**
32.	We have become nothing more than room-mates.	**True**	**False**
33.	I know my partner will never leave me.	**True**	**False**
34.	I am no longer proud of my body.	**True**	**False**
35.	My partner respects me.	**True**	**False**
36.	My partner constantly compares me to others.	**True**	**False**
37.	My partner still finds me desirable.	**True**	**False**
38.	We just seem to want different things.	**True**	**False**
39.	I am allowed to think for myself.	**True**	**False**
40.	I feel crowded by my partner.	**True**	**False**
41.	I am honest with my partner.	**True**	**False**
42.	People have no idea what our relationship is really like.	**True**	**False**
43.	My partner is open to suggestions.	**True**	**False**
44.	My partner has shut me out.	**True**	**False**
45.	My partner is my primary source of emotional support.	**True**	**False**
46.	I feel judged and rejected by my partner.	**True**	**False**
47.	My partner cares if I am upset or sad.	**True**	**False**
48.	My partner treats me like a child.	**True**	**False**
49.	My partner puts our relationship ahead of all others.	**True**	**False**
50.	I'll never satisfy my partner.	**True**	**False**
51.	My partner wants to hear my stories.	**True**	**False**

52. I chose my partner for the wrong reasons.	**True**	**False**
53. I look forward to our time together.	**True**	**False**
54. My partner thinks I am boring in bed.	**True**	**False**
55. My partner is lucky to have me.	**True**	**False**
56. My partner treats me like an employee.	**True**	**False**
57. I win my share of disputes.	**True**	**False**
58. I envy my friends' relationships.	**True**	**False**
59. My partner would protect me if necessary.	**True**	**False**
60. I am suspicious of my partner.	**True**	**False**
61. I feel needed by my partner.	**True**	**False**
62. My partner is jealous of me.	**True**	**False**

Scoring

How many even-numbered questions did you answer "True"? _____

How many odd-numbered questions did you answer "False"? _____

Add these two numbers to get your overall total.   _____

If your overall total is over 32, your relationship is probably in extreme danger of failing. If you scored 20 to 32, your relationship is seriously troubled. A total between 12 and 19 means your relationship is about average and needs work. If your overall total was from 0 to 11, your relationship is well above the norm, and may have isolated areas that need improvement.

GENERAL
RELATIONSHIP
PROBLEM
PROFILE

Before you continue, use the test that you just completed to identify the specific areas that are working against the health of your relationship. Use the space that follows here to list those even-numbered items to which you answered True and those odd-numbered items to which you answered False. For example, if you answered True to question 60, write here, "I am suspicious of my partner." If you answered False to question 61, write here, "I do not feel needed by my partner."

Now, based on the information you've uncovered, rank the following emotions in terms of presence and influence in your relationship. Let 1 designate the weakest emotion and 10 the strongest. In other words, the emotion that you rate a 10 is the most powerful emotion at work in your relationship at this time.

_____ Hostility/contempt

_____ Apathy

_____ Fear

_____ Distrust

_____ Hatred

_____ Love

_____ Loneliness

_____ Guilt/shame

_____ Anger

_____ Frustration

SPECIFIC
RELATIONSHIP
PROBLEM
PROFILE

The list that follows represents problem areas common to relationships in trouble. Some may apply to you. Some may not. Begin by circling every item on the list that plays a negative role in your relationship. Using the spaces to the left of the items, rank the problem areas, making 1 your worst problem area and going up from there. Use the spaces to the right of the items to write a sentence that describes the essence or core element of each problem.

_____ Trust _____

_____ Sex _____

_____ Money _____

_____ Family _____

_____ Time _____

_____ Children _____

_____ Lack of intimacy _____

_____ Communications _____

_____ Rage _____

_____ Drugs/alcohol _____

_____ Harshness _____

_____ Criticisms _____

_____ Fear _____

_____ Infidelity _____

_____ Boredom _____

_____ Lack of passion _____

_____ Jealousy _____

_____ Division of labor _____

_____ Communications _____

THE
RELATIONSHIP
BEHAVIOR
PROFILE:
YOUR
PARTNER

Continue the process of understanding and articulating how you feel about your partner and why. You may find some overlap from one question to another, but that's fine. Remember: The more honest and forthright you are, the better equipped you will be to address the problems that exist in your relationship today.

List five instances of your partner's loving behavior toward you during the last month.

1.

2.

3.

4.

5.

List five instances of unloving or hateful things your partner has done to you during the last month.

1.

2.

3.

4.

5.

List and describe your partner's five best qualities.

1.

2.

3.

4.

5.

List and describe your partner's five worst qualities.

1.

2.

3.

4.

5.

List five things that you have asked or scolded or nagged your partner to correct or improve, but that your partner has not corrected or
improved.

1.

2.

3.

4.

5.

List five things that made you fall in love with your partner.

1.

2.

3.

4.

5.

List five things that today would make you fall out of love with your partner.

1.

2.

3.

4.

5.

Describe your partner's sexual relationship with you, paying particular attention to your partner's

Pattern of initiation

Frequency

Quality

Problems

Describe your partner's tendency or lack thereof to focus on you, paying particular attention to his or her

Desire for being physically close

Desire to talk with you one-on-one

Desire to spend time alone with you

Desire to protect you or comfort you during times of need

Desire to please you

Do you look forward to seeing your partner at the end of a day? Answer "yes" or "no" here:_____. Now, in the space below, explain why you answered as you did. Be specific, honest, and thorough.

THE RELATIONSHIP BEHAVIOR PROFILE: YOU

You've given a status report on your partner in relationship to you. Now I want you to turn the tables. *Resolve right now not to lie to yourself*. It's not easy to face the truth, but anything less will only sabotage you. So go to it. Remember that this is *for your eyes only*.

List five instances of loving behavior toward your partner during the last month.

1.

2.

3.

4.

5.

List five instances of unloving or hateful things you have done to your partner during the last month.

1.

2.

3.

4.

5.

List and describe your five best qualities.

1.

2.

3.

4.

5.

List and describe your five worst qualities.

1.

2.

3.

4.

5.

List five things that your partner has asked or scolded or nagged you to correct or improve, but that you have not corrected or improved.

1.

2.

3.

4.

5.

List five things that made your partner fall in love with you.

1.

2.

3.

4.

5.

List five things that today would make your partner fall out of love with you.

1.

2.

3.

4.

5.

Describe your sexual relationship with your partner, paying particular attention to your own

Pattern of initiation

Frequency

Quality

Problems

Describe your tendency or lack thereof to focus on your partner, paying particular attention to your

Desire for being physically close

Desire to talk with your partner one-on-one

Desire to spend time alone with your partner

Desire to protect or comfort your partner during times of need

Desire to please your partner

Does your partner look forward to seeing you at the end of a day? Answer yes or no here:_____. Now, in the space below, explain why you answered as you did. Be specific, honest, and thorough.

YOUR
RELATIONSHIP
LIFESTYLE
PROFILE

The questions that follow focus on your relationship lifestyle—that is, the lifestyle you and your partner have negotiated between you. The answers to the questions will help to reveal the ways in which your lifestyle actually damages your relationship. Again, as always, be absolutely frank.

Do you and your partner have serious talks?	**Yes**	**No**
Do you talk mostly about problems?	**Yes**	**No**
Are the two of you generally pessimistic about how things in your life will work out?	**Yes**	**No**
Do you feel you are dominated by your kids?	**Yes**	**No**
By your work?	**Yes**	**No**
By housework?	**Yes**	**No**
By financial debt?	**Yes**	**No**
Do you feel out of shape?	**Yes**	**No**
Are you overweight?	**Yes**	**No**
Has your grooming or desire to look good around the house declined?	**Yes**	**No**
Do you find that you have very little energy?	**Yes**	**No**
Do you sit for extended periods of time watching TV?	**Yes**	**No**
Do you find it hard to keep your eyes open after supper?	**Yes**	**No**
Does one of you tend to already be asleep when the other comes to bed?	**Yes**	**No**
Do you go through long periods in which one or both of you are disinterested in sex, affection, or physical contact?	**Yes**	**No**
Are you easily bored with each other?	**Yes**	**No**

If people saw the two of you in public, would they describe you as looking or acting unhappy?   **Yes   No**

Are you turning toward others for comfort and entertainment?   **Yes   No**

Do the two of you drink more than you used to?   **Yes   No**
   Are you doing drugs of any kind?   **Yes   No**

Does each of you worry about the other getting the upper hand in the relationship, forcing you both to stay "on your guard" when you're together?   **Yes   No**

Do you make sure, when you do something in support of your partner, that he or she knows it and now owes you a favor—and does your partner do the same thing to you?   **Yes   No**

Do the two of you not know when to stop when an argument breaks out?   **Yes   No**

Do both of you tend to make harsh remarks and personal attacks when arguing?   **Yes   No**

Do the two of you often withdraw from each other instead of saying what is really on your minds?   **Yes   No**

Are you no longer interested in what interests your partner—and vice versa?   **Yes   No**

Do you think that you have behaviors or attitudes that, even though you know they are destructive, you don't wish to change for the good of the relationship?   **Yes   No**
   Are there similar behaviors or attitudes in your partner?   **Yes   No**

Even when you are your most loving toward your partner, is it hard for you to forget your negative feelings about him or her?	**Yes**	**No**
Do you think your partner feels the same way about you?	**Yes**	**No**
Have the two of you stopped talking about your future together?	**Yes**	**No**
What you two might be doing at retirement?	**Yes**	**No**
What you dream about?	**Yes**	**No**

RELATIONSHIP
COMMUNICATION
TEST

Lifestyle defines one way in which you and your partner relate. Communication defines another. The following quiz is designed to help you get in touch with your comfort level and patterns of communicating with the person who is supposed to be the most significant and trusted in your life. For each statement that expresses a problem that you perceive at least occasionally, circle "True."

1.	I often can't seem to find the right words to express what I want to say.	**True**	**False**
2.	I worry that exposing myself to my partner will result in rejection.	**True**	**False**
3.	I often don't talk because I'm afraid my opinion is wrong.	**True**	**False**
4.	Speaking up will only make things worse.	**True**	**False**
5.	I talk too much and don't give my partner a chance to speak.	**True**	**False**
6.	I don't look forward to talking to my partner.	**True**	**False**
7.	Once I get started in an argument, I have trouble stopping.	**True**	**False**
8.	My speech is often defensive.	**True**	**False**
9.	I frequently bring up his or her past failures.	**True**	**False**
10.	My actions don't match what I say.	**True**	**False**
11.	I don't really listen.	**True**	**False**

12. I try to repay anger with anger or insult with insult. **True** **False**
13. I tease my mate too much. **True** **False**
14. I talk about really important things too rarely. **True** **False**
15. I often lie by omission. **True** **False**
16. I hate it when my partner brings up a problem. **True** **False**
17. I think it's important to lay out to my partner all of the complaints I have about him or her. **True** **False**
18. I state my complaints in a heated manner. **True** **False**
19. I tend to say "You always" or "You never" when discussing my complaints with my partner. **True** **False**
20. I rarely state my complaints, to keep from hurting my spouse. **True** **False**
21. I don't like to argue because I feel arguing reflects badly on the relationship. **True** **False**
22. I don't like to discuss our negative feelings because it only makes us feel worse. **True** **False**
23. I don't feel I should have to bring up what's bothering me because my partner should already know. **True** **False**

Take a moment to look over your answers. This will help you as you continue with the following test.

CHEMISTRY TEST In an intimate relationship, no discussion of relationship lifestyle is complete without including sex. Don't delude yourself with an "It's not that important" attitude. It is that important, because it can be one of the first aspects of a relationship to reveal trouble in the works. So complete the following quiz as truthfully as you possibly can.

1. I am no longer physically attracted to my partner. **True** **False**
2. My partner makes me feel sexy. **True** **False**

3.	My partner and I no longer kiss and caress.	**True**	**False**
4.	Sex with my partner is energetic and satisfying.	**True**	**False**
5.	My partner and I no longer flirt with each other.	**True**	**False**
6.	My partner and I would rather be together alone than with other people.	**True**	**False**
7.	I no longer look my partner in the eye when we are alone together.	**True**	**False**
8.	If we do not have sex every few days, I really begin to miss it.	**True**	**False**
9.	At various times I resent my partner.	**True**	**False**
10.	I love to give my partner physical pleasure.	**True**	**False**

Scoring

Put a check mark next to each odd-numbered statement to which you answered "True." How many are checked?   _____

Put an X next to each even-numbered statement to which you answered "False." How many are X'd?   _____

Add the two totals together. If your overall total is more than 3, you have problems with the intimate/sexual aspect of your relationship. You've just created a valuable tool for later planning.

THE FIVE
TOUGH
QUESTIONS

Your answers to the following questions are *for your eyes only*. This is your opportunity to express the worst and darkest of your feelings about your partner, yourself, and your relationship. Be ruthlessly honest. You will only shortchange your future if you choose to deny what is really going on in your relationship right now.

1. Considering that at least one definition of love is that the security and well-being of your partner is as significant to you as your own security and well-being, then would you say that,

based on results, you behave in a way that indicates that you are in love with your partner? Why?

2. Using that same definition, is your partner in love with you? Why?

3. Knowing what you now know about your relationship, would you still get involved with the same person if you had to do it all over again? Why?

4. When comparing yourself to other people in relationships, do you feel that you have been cheated or have settled too cheaply? Why?

5. If you could break off your relationship or get a divorce from your partner right now without any inconvenience, legal costs, or embarrassment, and without any undue hardship on your children (if you have any), would you do it? Why?

The truth may not be easy, but it's the first, exciting step toward making that crucial U-turn that your relationship demands. Go back and look over what you've done so far. Then take the next step.

chapter 3

BLOWING UP THE MYTHS

We all enter our adult lives with expectations. We've been taught and have believed a complicated set of rules and "supposed-to-be" truths that set us up for disappointment. Life isn't logical; relationships don't follow fairy-tale story lines. And when reality catches up with us, we think we've failed at the game of life and love. Well, the bad news is that those expectations were never realistic in the first place, and the so-called rules of life-as-it-ought-to-be were nothing more than myths. The good news is that once you truly understand this, you can get busy replacing myths with a reality-based mindset. You're about to work through what I consider to be ten of the most dangerous relationship myths common to today's attitudes. Be open to rethinking each of these myths. Search honestly for the degree to which each has affected your view of yourself and your relationship. And ready yourself for a vital step in the process of change.

Myth #1——A MEETING OF THE MINDS

It may be appealing to believe that two people could come to a complete understanding of each other, but it has no basis in reality. Every one of us is one-of-a-kind, and when you add to that some differences in how our respective genders are "wired up," you're talking about a significant amount of territory that we don't and never will hold in common with our partners. Every pair of partners shares a mix of similarities and differences that may or may not change but will never resolve into each seeing through the eyes of the other. Right now, take some time to appreciate what's *real*. Using the exercises that follow, remember how you and your partner "fit," and reconsider the ways that you don't.

THE "NATURAL" FIT

Let's start with what the two of you brought to your first meeting. List at least ten ways you're compatible that existed before you even had a chance to get to know each other. These will probably include common backgrounds, tastes, or activities. They may include personality traits, what makes you laugh, ideals, or intellectual interests. Be as specific as you can. If you can think of more than ten, write those down, too.

1.

2.

3.

4.

5.

6.

7.

8.

9.

10.

THE
"ADJUSTED"
FIT

Presumably, you've been with your partner for some years. The common ground you shared at your first meeting has had time to grow and deepen. Consider the years that have passed since you've been together. How have you developed or discovered new ways to be compatible? List at least ten ways you are compatible that have grown over time. These might include knowing mutual friends, having children, liking the same activities, or having similar travel interests. They may include vocational or spiritual ties and pursuits.

1.

2.

3.

4.

5.

6.

7.

8.

9.

10.

"THANKS FOR THE DIFFERENCES . . ." By now, you've remembered that you do indeed share a limited meeting of minds and spirits with your partner. But you and I both know that you also share quite a few differences. Make a list of ten differences between the two of you.

1.

2.

3.

4.

5.

6.

7.

8.

9.

10.

Read over the list you've just created. Put a check mark to the left of each item that could be considered "gender-specific." (Reread pages 40 to 43 in *Relationship Rescue* if you're having trouble identifying which these might be.) Then, in the space provided after each numbered item, imagine and describe at least one way that the difference is or could be complementary—that is, something that makes your relationship richer, more dynamic, more effective, or more interesting, or that enhances each individual's traits.

Myth #2——A GREAT ROMANCE

So you started out with orchestras playing, fireworks lighting up the sky, and a nonstop silly grin on your face? You thought you had died and gone to super-hero heaven? Get over it. All that sizzle and snap had its place in your long-term relationship, but it was only one of many potential phases, and without fail, the least likely to linger over a lifetime. The fact that it ever happened to you is a gift in the first place, and it's a gift you can continue to enjoy, even after the emotions evolve into something deeper and more lasting. You need to reconnect to what was at the heart of all the headiness and accept the growing process as an extension of a great gift.

FALLING IN
LOVE

Put yourself back in time and conjure up exactly who it was that you got so syrupy about. Write a paragraph describing your partner as the person you fell in love with: Describe him or her physically, emotionally, spiritually, financially, and intellectually. Use plenty of descriptive detail—make it so that if I were to read what you wrote, I could "see" your partner as he or she appeared in the heady first days of your infatuation.

BEING IN
LOVE

You've just described your partner in probably the most romantic and idealistic terms you will ever conceive in the history of your relationship. Some of what you saw in your partner was unrealistic. Some of it was the short-term stuff of courtship. But some of what you saw has to do with the core person with whom you have formed a relationship. Go back now to what you just wrote.

1. Put a line through any characteristic that you know is truly unrealistic.
2. Underline each characteristic that is typical of puppy love or infatuation but that would not necessarily continue into a more mature love.
3. Finally, circle each characteristic that was true about your partner at the time and could reasonably continue over the lifetime of a relationship. Write each circled characteristic in the space below. Put a check mark beside any item that still describes your partner. If any item does not continue to describe your partner, answer the question, "Why not? What happened to change this about my partner?"

Myth #3——GREAT PROBLEM SOLVING

You already know that I'm a firm believer in agreeing to disagree. Some of the basic disagreements in a relationship can never be resolved unless one partner or the other sacrifices true beliefs or intrinsic personality traits. That resolution is not what a good relationship is all about. We'll deal later with some fundamental tools for dealing with differences. For now, I want you to get in touch with the specific areas that consistently raise conflicts in your relationship. This will provide you with valuable reference material later on.

WHAT ARE WE FIGHTING ABOUT?

Following is a checklist of some common themes for conflict in long-term relationships. For each item that applies in some way to your relationship, put a check mark in the space to the left of the item. Once you've checked each theme that applies to you and your partner, rate the checked items in the spaces to the right according to their relative importance in your relationship (1 = hardly a problem, 3 = bothersome, 5 = extremely troubling).

_____ Sex
_____ Raising children
_____ Disciplining children
_____ Allocating money
_____ Allocating time
_____ Religious beliefs
_____ Religious observances
_____ In-laws
_____ Hobbies
_____ Entertaining at home
_____ Same-gender friendships
_____ Opposite-gender friendships
_____ Neatness at home
_____ Planning for the future
_____ Job choice
_____ Job schedule
_____ Language use
_____ Driving style
_____ Leisure activities
_____ Promptness

_____ Physical affection
_____ Communication
_____ Courtesy
_____ Choice of food
_____ Alcohol-drinking habits
_____ Community involvement

I THINK . . .
I FEEL

Now that you've identified some of your perennial areas of conflict with your partner, list five such areas that you rated a 5. If you don't have that many that rated a 5, choose what you consider the most important issues that you rated lower.

Area of Conflict	Issue	Emotion

Finish the chart. For each item you listed, first identify the issue. (What specifically about this area of your shared life turns it into a conflict?) Next, identify the emotions underlying the issue. (What *at heart* do you feel in the midst of this conflict? Fear? Hurt? Betrayal? Rejection?) Give this some time. Don't settle for superficial answers. Be specific, gutsy, and thorough.

Finally, copy each item below and answer this question in the space under it: "What could you or your partner do that would let you agree to disagree on this?"

1.

2.

3.

4.

5.

Myth #4—COMMON INTERESTS THAT BOND YOU TOGETHER FOREVER

I believe that every couple in an intimate relationship has at least one compelling interest in common, and that is their partnership. But too many people add stress and pain to a relatively good relationship because they buy into the myth that a couple should do everything together. So let's get to the heart of the matter. What really counts between the two of you?

A WISH LIST   Describe one interest, hobby, or activity that you wish you had in common with your partner.

REALITY
CHECK
Now, this is important. Look at what you've just described, and dig under the surface of it. If the two of you shared this interest, hobby, or activity, what would it add to the quality of your relationship? List three underlying values in the interest or activity you described that can be shared with your partner without that common interest as the vehicle. After each value, answer this question: "How can we make this value part of our relationship without participating in the activity?"

1.

2.

3.

Myth #5——A PEACEFUL RELATIONSHIP

Arguing in a relationship is neither a virtue nor an evil. It is an inevitability for any relationship that is going to grow and deepen over a lifetime. *How* you argue, on the other hand, can certainly produce good or bad results in your relationship. Think of the worst argument you can ever remember having with your partner. Look with complete honesty at yourself. Remember, *you* are responsible for *you* in this equation. What you acknowledge, you can change. And as you change, you can become an inspiring force for your partner. Finish the following exercises with courage.

THE RULES OF
THE RING

Circle "True" to identify every statement that could describe you in the midst of arguing with your partner.

I cut my partner off in midsentence.	**True**	**False**
I out-scream my partner.	**True**	**False**
I rarely apologize.	**True**	**False**
I demand that my partner admit that I'm right.	**True**	**False**
I pull others (children, parents, friends) into our personal arguments.	**True**	**False**

I bring up past hurts and angers.	**True**	**False**
I walk out before the argument is over.	**True**	**False**
I resort to tears.	**True**	**False**
I resort to name calling.	**True**	**False**
I "gunny-sack" my feelings rather than have them erupt on the spot.	**True**	**False**
I pick fights for the exhilaration of it.	**True**	**False**
I go ballistic when I don't score points.	**True**	**False**
I retreat into silence when an argument erupts.	**True**	**False**
I make threats.	**True**	**False**
I insist on having the last word.	**True**	**False**
I resort to physical acts in my anger.	**True**	**False**
I throw down ultimatums.	**True**	**False**

The more statements above to which you gave a "True" answer, the more work you have ahead of you. You can learn to argue in a manner that actually serves your relationship, but first you have to admit to what's really going on now.

SIMMER, SPEW, OR BLOW THE LID OFF

Read the four definitions that follow. Each describes a destructive interactive style in arguments. Based on the true-false quiz you just took, rate the following from 1 to 4, with 1 being the definition that most closely describes you in a fight with your partner and a 4 next to the one that least describes you.

_____ Attack Reaction
You tend to quickly abandon issues of disagreement and instead attack the worth of your partner.

_____ Gunny Sack Reaction
You do not achieve emotional closure at the end of an argument and the emotions come bubbling out later.

_____ Overreaction
You tend to react with disproportionate emotion to an isolated event.

_____ Cumulative Reaction
You tend to react explosively in an argument after "biting your tongue" in a prior series of related or unrelated confrontations.

Myth #6—THE COMPLETE VENTING OF FEELINGS

I've said again and again that total honesty is a foundational necessity if you are ever going to put yourself and your relationship on the right track. Please remember, however, that as you've worked here on facing the truth of your relationship in this workbook, I've also stressed that what you write here is *for your eyes only*. Why? Because while you are expressing what seems to be the truth at the time, you may actually just be getting the big, distracting emotions out of your system. We call that venting. It can be helpful to you because it can free you to then dig in a more rational manner for the balanced reality. But when you vent your exaggerated emotions on your partner, you run the risk of saying destructive things that can never be unsaid and losing your credibility as a truth teller. The following exercises are designed to help you identify the role that venting plays in your relationship.

WHAT'S YOUR STYLE?

List five specific occasions when you indulged in venting. These may be physical acts or verbal attacks. Maybe you haven't been as dramatic as Karen (see pages 52 to 53 of *Relationship Rescue*), or maybe you have. Don't let yourself off easy. You may have to give this some thought before you see how it applies to you.

1.

2.

3.

4.

5.

WHAT'S YOUR   List five specific occasions when your partner indulged in venting.
PARTNER'S
STYLE?

1.

2.

3.

4.

5.

PING-PONG   For each of the listed "venting events," describe the outcome—
that is, the immediate effect it had on your relationship in terms
of

Action, reaction, and counterreaction

Trust, closeness, and understanding

Subsequent ability to disagree in a constructive manner

Myth #7——NOTHING TO DO WITH SEX

Whoever came up with the idea that a great relationship does not in some way depend on sex must have been living on some other planet. An intimate relationship is, *by definition*, one that has a uniquely sexual element to it. When problems grow between partners, sex is one of the first aspects of their relationship to be affected. And the farther from a mutually satisfying physical experience they travel, the closer to center stage the sexual issue moves. I want you to get real about your physical relationship. Own up to what is going on and why. With this information will come the power to change a less-than-satisfying sexual experience with your mate.

JUST THE FACTS   How often is sexual intimacy a part of your relationship? (Numerous times a day? Once a week? Twice a year? Be as accurate and realistic as possible.)

Which of you usually initiates sexual intimacy?

Typically, how does that person initiate sexual intimacy?

How does the less-frequent initiator typically do so?

Under what circumstances do you and your partner engage in sexual intimacy?

How would you describe your sex life with your partner? (*Be honest, but never, never share this with your partner!*)

Physically:

Emotionally:

Mentally:

Review the answers you gave above. What, if anything, would you change about your sexual relationship if you could?

ONCE UPON A TIME   Write a paragraph describing in detail the high point (that is, the most satisfying expression) of your sexual relationship with your partner. Include when, where, how often, who initiated it, how he or she initiated it, how satisfying you found it, how free you felt in the midst of it, and any other pertinent details.

CHEMICAL REACTIONS   In the paragraph that you just completed, underline any aspect of the sexual experience that does not usually happen today in your relationship. Circle any aspect of the experience that does usually happen today. What happened between then and now to change your experience?

Myth #8—YOU CANNOT SURVIVE A FLAWED PARTNER

There's an old saying: "If you find the perfect church, don't join it. You'll wreck it!" Meaning? Every one of us comes with quirks, idiosyncrasies, flaws, and personal peccadilloes. No exceptions. We often characterize our own unusual traits in positive terms. Our partners may not fare as well in our estimation. On a good day, most of us are prepared to say that the ever-present human oddities are part of what makes life in the human race vibrant and dynamic—as long as we don't have to live in the same house with them. I hope you see the gap in logic there. I want you to take a look at yourself in this regard. Treat this subject with respect— you may be tempted to make a joke of it (that's a defense mechanism, by the way). Don't. Be honest and thorough.

IF I WERE YOU . . .

Begin by writing at least one paragraph that describes your traits as a roommate or housemate. Be sure to include your most endearing traits as a partner; your most aggravating traits as a partner; and your most bizarre traits as a partner.

Now write how you would like your partner to view and describe you as a roommate or housemate. Remember: You should still be talking about the same person, with all the traits you described above.

Imagine your partner describing you with sympathy, affection, humor, appreciation, tolerance, and loyalty. How would it sound?

Myth #9—A RIGHT WAY AND A WRONG WAY

I might define this myth as a profound lack of imagination. The very idea that there is only one way to create anything as complex and colorful as a relationship between two people is ridiculous. Yet many people seem at some level to believe this, and they pay a steep price in disillusionment and disappointment. If you genuinely want to rescue your relationship, you will have to learn how to focus on what works. That means opening your eyes to a wider range of possibilities, embracing a more creative approach to relating to your partner, and laying aside arbitrary mindsets that simply do not work.

THE "PERFECT" COUPLE

Take some time to think over the relationships, other than your own, that you've had an opportunity to watch in action. Identify three couples you know who appear to be in a happy or "successful" long-term relationship.

1.

2.

3.

For each of the couples you have named, use the space provided to describe three examples of their success (actions, style of exchange, signs of affection, lifestyle, mutual or individual activities, and so on). Be on the lookout for aspects of their relationship that you would not have associated with a good relationship—look specifically for aspects that surprise you.

Myth #10—WHEN YOU GET YOUR PARTNER STRAIGHTENED OUT

This myth brings us back to one of the most crucial truths at work in your life and your relationship. You are *responsible*, no matter who is to blame. You are the most important person in this relationship. You must be the focus of your efforts to change. The exercise to follow will help you begin to see how this process of honest assessment can add up to positive change.

MIRROR, MIRROR Go back to pages 4 to 9 in this workbook and review your answers to "The Best People," "In a Perfect World, Who Are You?" and "In Reality, What Are You Doing?" From your answers to these exercises, extract one negative trait that you have identified about your-self. Describe in detail one actual situation or event with your partner in which this negative trait showed itself in destructive action.

Now imagine that you can return to that situation or event and "rewrite the script." List at least five ways that you could have altered the outcome of the situation by changing your attitude, actions, reactions, tone of voice, body language, or other behavior.

1.

2.

3.

4.

5.

chapter 4

ELIMINATING YOUR BAD SPIRIT

I hope after reading Chapter 4 of *Relationship Rescue*, you're convinced that everyone, including you, has an irrational and destructive side to their personalities. You can't afford to ignore or deny it if you want to create the relationship that you most desire. In the exercise that follows, I've provided ten scored checklists—one for each of ten "bad spirit" characteristics. As you read the items that characterize each bad spirit, examine yourself for how closely they describe you in relationship with your partner, and give yourself a score for each. Take this seriously, and give it your best, most honest effort. You can't change what you do not acknowledge.

Scoring

1 = Never
2 = Seldom
3 = Sometimes
4 = Often
5 = Always

Characteristic #1: You're a Scorekeeper

	1	2	3	4	5
You tend to keep score of things your partner does, such as leisure activities, outings with friends, hours with the children, and chores completed.					
You make sure your partner never gets the upper hand and never gets by with a "freebie."					
You bank "points" that you hold over your partner's head for leverage.					
You make concessions in a negotiating fashion rather than offering them as a gift of support.					
You seldom if ever do something in support of your partner without making sure that he or she knows it, including a detailed explanation of the imposition it created for you.					
In any type of dispute or confrontation with your partner, you actively seek outside allies in the form of family and friends in an effort to shift the balance of power.					
You insist on having the last word or final act of defiance.					
Total the numbers in each column here.					
Total the five totals for a grand total here.					

Characteristic #2: You're a Fault Finder

	1	2	3	4	5
You seldom if ever let an infraction by your partner slide by, regardless of how trivial.					
You find yourself saying to your partner such things as, "You should have known better." "You should have helped me out when I was stressed." "You should have done what I wanted without my having to ask you."					
You tend to say "always" and "never" when criticizing your partner. "You always do this." "You never help me out in the kitchen." "You always ignore me."					
You tend to complain about how you're not getting what you deserve or that life is unfair to you—an attitude that you quickly transfer to your partner, as if he or she is to blame.					
You counterattack with criticism whenever you're being criticized.					
You are obsessively interested in getting your partner to admit to wrongdoing rather than listening to what your partner has to say.					
Total the numbers in each column here.					
Total the five totals for a grand total here.					

Characteristic #3: You Think It's Your Way or the Highway

	1	2	3	4	5
You are intolerant of your partner's initiatives or ideas.					
You regularly interrupt your partner during conversations so that you can get in what you want to say instead of patiently allowing your partner to finish what he or she has to say.					
You "change the game" on those few occasions when you realize that your partner is making a good point.					
You cannot end a confrontation until your partner acknowledges that you are right.					
If your partner won't admit the rightness of your position, you tend to sulk or act like a martyr, making sure your partner understands that you don't feel appreciated.					
You regularly assume a saintly, pious position with friends and family, telling them about all you have to put up with, about how your partner is impossible to live with.					
You tend to start sentences with guilt-inducing phrases like "If you loved me . . ." or "If you cared for me . . ." or with "I told you so; you should've listened."					
Total the numbers in each column here.					
Total the five totals for a grand total here.					

Characteristic #4: You Turn into an Attack Dog

	1	2	3	4	5
Your interactions are marked by, at the least, a very harsh tone of voice and often by "in-your-face" shouting.					
Your interactions are marked by such body language as a curled upper lip, a pointed finger in the face, or a deliberate Clint Eastwood–type "killer stare" or exaggerated eye rolling.					
Your comments are laden with condescension or sarcasm, as in, "Well, you really turned out to be a great catch!"					
Your comments are full of insults and name calling, from "bitch" and "bastard" to "fat" and "ugly."					
Your comments are filled with "you" statements such as: "You make me sick." "You disgust me." "You are stupid and worthless."					
You purposely and pointedly attack your partner's vulnerable areas and values.					
As opposed to an act of overt commission, you withhold from your partner that which you know they want and need in order to have peace in their life.					
You seek to manage your partner with intimidation, both physical and mental/emotional.					

	1	2	3	4	5
Total the numbers in each column here.					
Total the five totals for a grand total here.					

Characteristic #5: You Are a Passive Warmonger

	1	2	3	4	5
After listening to your partner make a suggestion, you agree with the suggestion, then a few minutes later start talking about why the suggestion will fail rather than how it could succeed.					
You feign confusion when your partner explains even simple rationales for changing something in your relationship that you happen to like.					
You feign ineptness over activities that you don't like to do—painting a room of the house, for instance, or putting a child to bed.					
You time vague and subjectively defined "illnesses" or come up with competing events to interfere with plans made by your partner that you don't like.					
You often start sentences with the phrase "Yeah, but . . ."					
Total the numbers in each column here.					
Total the five totals for a grand total here.					

Characteristic #6: You Resort to Smoke and Mirrors

	1	2	3	4	5
Your interactions constantly focus on superficial and trivial topics.					
Your interactions that begin to approach the real issues are disrupted by anger, abrupt changes of subject, or withdrawal.					
You tend to talk passionately about the problems of other people that mirror what is really bothering you, but when confronted, you deny their relevance.					
You find yourself becoming very defensive if your partner directly asks you if there is anything bothering you.					
You are a master of defensiveness. You always know how to direct attention away from yourself if the questions get too personal.					
Total the numbers in each column here.					
Total the five totals for a grand total here.					

Characteristic #7: You Will Not Forgive

	1	2	3	4	5
You are consumed with such anger at your partner that you'll explode over the smallest disagreements or difficulty.					
You feel so bitter that you take a pessimistic view of life in general.					
Your body feels so physically unbalanced—the condition is called *heterostasis*—that you often experience sleep disturbances, nightmares, poor concentration, and fatigue. You develop severe headaches, back spasms, even heart attacks—all because your body's chemical balance is dramatically disrupted because of your stress.					
You cannot read a book or watch a television show or movie without finding something in it that reminds you of your resentment.					
You keep in your memory bank all the imperfections in your partner, you remember all of the mistakes and failures he or she has made, and you bring them up constantly.					
You interpret many statements and actions of your partner in a negative fashion, based on the slimmest thread of evidence or often no evidence at all.					

	1	2	3	4	5
You think you shouldn't yet forgive your partner because he or she is not acting sorry or apologetic enough.					
You think you shouldn't yet forgive your partner because he or she has not done enough things for you in order to pay penance.					
You try to control your partner through shame rather than seeking to inspire your partner.					
Total the numbers in each column here.					
Total the five totals for a grand total here.					

Characteristic #8: You Are the Bottomless Pit

	1	2	3	4	5
You talk yourself out of friendships and relationships because you think the person you like is out of your league.					
You fear rejection for voicing an opinion. You'd rather not say something than risk the disapproval of others, and when you do talk, you wonder if you're making the right impression.					
You find yourself saying "Thank you" or "I'm sorry" frequently and unnecessarily.					

	1	2	3	4	5
You talk yourself out of trying something new with your partner, from horseback riding to counseling, because you don't want to look stupid.					
When you are complimented, you immediately downplay whatever you did that led to the compliment.					
When you buy presents for others, you worry if they are "right" or "good enough."					
You state your beliefs as questions, asking your partner what he or she feels about certain subjects that are important to you instead of declaring your position and taking a stand.					
Instead of expressing anger, you become tearful and play the victim.					
You are so sensitive and thin-skinned about any criticism that your partner cannot tease you or joke with you, and he or she sure as heck can't tell you the truth when you need to hear it.					
No matter what the question with regard to making plans, your answer is always the same: "I don't know, I don't care. Whatever you want to do."					
Total the numbers in each column here.					
Total the five totals for a grand total here.					

Characteristic #9: You're Too Comfortable

	1	2	3	4	5
You never talk about such subjects as where your relationship is going, what your deepest desires are, what you dream about, what gives you passion.					
You're tired even after a good night's sleep, and you find it hard to keep your eyes open after dinner.					
You sit for extended periods of time watching television.					
You say to yourself you can't do things because you don't have the willpower.					
Your first reaction to almost any suggestion by your partner is "No."					
You don't have the desire to go somewhere new or try something that is not part of the regular routine of your life.					
You definitely avoid anything involving risk to your current lifestyle. As a result, your lifestyle offers no challenge and no stimulation.					
You feel emotional talk is bothersome and sort of silly. You always roll your eyes when you hear someone say, "Why don't you express your feelings?"					

	1	2	3	4	5
You answer too many questions with "I don't know." What you're really saying is that you have closed your mind and decided it's not worth the work anymore of trying to understand what's happening to you.					
Total the numbers in each column here.					
Total the five totals for a grand total here.					

Characteristic #10: You've Given Up

	1	2	3	4	5
You have consciously accepted a dull pain as a way of life.					
You feel a regular sense of malaise or lack of energy.					
You have surrendered to the reality of just "going through the motions" in a motionless relationship.					
You often think or say, "What's the use? It will never change."					
You no longer even bother to protest when attacked or abused by your partner.					
You think it's pointless to try to change because it will only make your partner angry.					

	1	2	3	4	5
You feel lonely.					
You have begun to turn to other people or activities in search of fulfillment.					
You express disappointment in the relationship covertly, constantly becoming "ill," for instance, and having to spend days in bed, or even turning to prescription pills or alcohol or twice-a-week sessions with therapists.					
Total the numbers in each column here.					
Total the five totals for a grand total here.					

ADDING IT UP   You have invaluable information at your fingertips in the preceding charts. To bring this raw material into clearer focus, summarize what you've uncovered by transferring your grand totals to the list that follows. Remember: This information can become powerful knowledge.

_____ Characteristic #1: You're a Scorekeeper
_____ Characteristic #2: You're a Fault Finder
_____ Characteristic #3: You Think It's Your Way or the Highway
_____ Characteristic #4: You Turn into an Attack Dog
_____ Characteristic #5: You Are a Passive Warmonger
_____ Characteristic #6: You Resort to Smoke and Mirrors
_____ Characteristic #7: You Will Not Forgive
_____ Characteristic #8: You Are the Bottomless Pit
_____ Characteristic #9: You're Too Comfortable
_____ Characteristic #10: You've Given Up

This is an opportunity for you to gain profound self-knowledge about the way that you continually sabotage yourself and your relationship. Look at the list you just created. The higher the number to the right of each characteristic, the more pervasive that bad spirit is in your life. In order to see yourself more clearly, copy the list to the chart below, writing the highest scoring characteristic first, the next-highest second, and so forth. As you write each characteristic, change it to become a sentence in the first person. For example, the first characteristic would read, "I'm a scorekeeper," the second would read, "I'm a fault finder," and so on.

Characteristic	Total Score

Characteristic	Total Score

part iii

DISCOVER THE POTENTIAL

Before you begin this portion of the *Relationship Rescue Workbook*, read or reread Chapters 5 through 8 of *Relationship Rescue*.

chapter 5

RECLAIMING YOUR CORE — THE PERSONAL
RELATIONSHIP VALUES

Whether you realize it or not, you've made some significant strides toward a new relationship with your partner in the previous two sections of this workbook. You've dug under the layers of faulty attitudes and destructive patterns of behavior to glimpse a better, truer you. You've also taken a clear-eyed look at how your relationship has been struggling and diagnosed some of the specific problems that will need to be addressed before you can enjoy a better life together. Now you're ready to begin the process of reprogramming and strategizing for the relationship you want. Don't shortchange yourself or your partner by giving the work ahead anything but your best in time, energy, and focus. You can make a fresh start that comes from a place of strength and integrity—if you're ready and willing to invest yourself wholly and honestly. When you change, your relationship will change. Exciting prospect? It's yours for the taking.

You have all it takes within you to reprogram yourself for success—integrity, honesty, compassion, enthusiasm—and you have the ability to adopt the proper spirit that will start the reconnection process with your partner. As you work through the ten Personal Relationship Values that follow, take the time and give the energy to find each one within you and shake it awake.

Personal Relationship Value #1—

OWN YOUR RELATIONSHIP

You may get tired of hearing it, but I'll never get tired of repeating it. You are fully accountable for your relationship. You have created your experience. You not only choose your own actions and attitudes, but also your reactions to your partner. The good news is that you can choose differently from now on. But as always, you have to acknowledge what exists right now before you can change it.

"WHINE WARNING" Give some thought now to your own list of "whines." Identify five specific aspects of your relationship in which you feel that you are not in control but rather a victim, "stuck" because of your partner's attitudes or behavior. List each of these aspects in the spaces that follow.

1.

2.

3.

4.

5.

QUIZ   Choose one item from the list you just created, and copy it here. I'd suggest that you pick out the one that bothers you the most. Then answer each of the questions below as thoroughly and honestly as you can in relation to the item you selected.

1. What payoff are you giving your partner in this circumstance?

2. Are you being unassertive in a way that makes your partner feel that you can be taken advantage of?

3. What are you doing that keeps you and your partner from dealing with this issue?

4. What are you doing to enable this behavior in your partner?

5. What can you do to help him or her to genuinely change?

Once you're satisfied that you've examined the "whine" as thoroughly as you can, choose another and repeat the questions (you can use extra paper for this, but save it with the workbook for later reference). Do this until you've examined every item from the list you made above.

PERSONAL
STATEMENT
Do you believe that this personal relationship value is true? Make it your own right now by writing it out as a sentence with you as the subject.

Personal Relationship Value #2—
ACCEPT THE RISK OF VULNERABILITY

If you do as I say and let yourself feel again in your relationship despite past hurts and disappointments, will you get hurt? Possibly. But not necessarily. However, you can be sure that if you continue to hide and protect yourself from vulnerability, you will doom yourself to a relationship that can only get worse. You do not need to be ruled by your fear. You can face the outcome of change, and the outcome may be the best thing that ever happened to you.

"I'M AFRAID THAT . . ." Reflect on what you've discovered so far about your part in creating your present situation. That information contains some vital clues about what keeps you from changing a bad situation, and I'm willing to bet that those reasons include a hefty amount of fear. I want you to nail it. Create a list of five fears that have contributed to your past decisions, behavior, characteristics, or spirit in the relationship.

1.

2.

3.

4.

5.

"WHAT IF . . . ?" The fears that you just identified may have some basis in reality. That's okay. You can break through the paralysis that fear produces by facing the fear squarely. Write out each of the five fears you identified above as you imagine them playing out in your relationship. What if each of the fears came true? What would happen? Spell it out for yourself here.

What if . . . ?
Then . . .

What if . . . ?
Then . . .

What if . . . ?
Then . . .

What if . . . ?
Then . . .

What if . . . ?

Then . . .

"AND THEN I WOULD . . ."   Now finish each story, remembering what Value #1 taught you: You are not a victim. Suppose the worst happened. What would you do about it? Suggest three possible responses you could make if each of your fears were realized.

    1.

       a.

       b.

       c.

2.

   a.

   b.

   c.

3.

   a.

b.

c.

4.

a.

b.

c.

5.

a.

b.

c.

Personal Relationship Value #3—
ACCEPT YOUR PARTNER

Your partner's number-one need in life is to be accepted. If you did not know it before, you know it now. And he or she deserves to have that need met by the number-one person in his or her life—you. Acceptance of the person does not mean acceptance of every attitude or behavior. It does mean valuing the human being and looking for what is worthy, vulnerable, and good. You can do this for your partner, but if you've developed a negative spirit, you'll need some practice. Start here.

INVENTORY 1:
MY TOP TEN
PARTNER
GRIPES

Let's first clear out the negatives that may be getting in the way of your feeling and communicating acceptance to your partner. Quickly identify the top ten on your list of complaints against your partner.

1.

2.

3.

4.

5.

6.

7.

8.

9.

10.

INVENTORY 2:
MY PARTNER'S
TOP TWENTY
POSITIVES

Feel better? I hope so, because I want you to let that list go now. Just take a deep breath, remember that you are on the road to change, and let the gripes go. Now you're ready to get serious about appreciating the person with whom you have chosen to share a life. Identify the top twenty characteristics in your partner that you appreciate. This may be more difficult and take longer than the complaints. List as many as you can in one sitting. If you truly run dry, give it a few days. Spend time thinking about it and observing your partner until you can fill the list.

1.

2.

3.

4.

5.

6.

7.

8.

9.

10.

11.

12.

13.

14.

15.

16.

17.

18.

19.

20.

THE WHINE RATIO Now consider your "whine ratio" with your partner. Read the following statements and circle the appropriate answers.

I am quick to lose patience and show it when my partner lets me down.	**True**	**False**
My partner doesn't listen unless I use a verbal two by four.	**True**	**False**
I can't remember the last compliment I paid my partner.	**True**	**False**
When my partner disagrees with me, I tend to think I'm right and my partner is wrong.	**True**	**False**
I am more likely to offer feedback when I'm upset than when I'm pleased.	**True**	**False**
I find it easier to offer praise to friends than to my partner.	**True**	**False**
I honestly feel that if I don't tell my partner what he or she is doing wrong, he or she won't have a clue.	**True**	**False**
I don't believe in "holding my tongue" where my partner is concerned.	**True**	**False**
I'd rather "score a point" in a disagreement with my partner than understand his or her point of view.	**True**	**False**
I used to see more positive traits in my partner than I do now.	**True**	**False**
I feel the need to defend myself when my friends praise my partner.	**True**	**False**
I fear that if I praise my partner, it will be used against me later.	**True**	**False**
I believe that compliments just feed my partner's overblown ego.	**True**	**False**
I enjoy complaining about my partner to my friends.	**True**	**False**
I feel that making "more" of my partner in some way makes "less" of me.	**True**	**False**

It's important to me that friends and family know my partner's faults so that they can understand what I have to live with.	**True**	**False**
If I received more compliments from my partner, I would offer more in return.	**True**	**False**
I believe that my partner learns more from constructive criticism than from praise.	**True**	**False**
The "good news" about my partner honestly doesn't occur to me.	**True**	**False**
I am basically pessimistic about my partner's potential for positive change.	**True**	**False**

Scoring

Score yourself by adding up the number of times you answered "True."

0 to 4   You have a better than average whine ratio; why not make the best of it by eliminating the whine altogether?

5 to 9   You are roughly average in your attitude toward your partner, which is not good enough for a great relationship.

10 to 14   You need a major overhaul of your perspective.

15 to 20   You have almost entirely deprived your partner of a basic human need: affection and approval from his or her life partner.

Personal Relationship Value #4—
FOCUS ON THE FRIENDSHIP

The greatest hope for your relationship is a return to the friendship that drew you to your partner in the first place. Take a step away from your present problems and give friendship a closer look. Then let the clock roll back to those early days, and remember the specifics of your friendship with your partner before your relationship got into trouble.

WHAT I WANT
IN A FRIEND

Begin by calling to mind the people in your life *other* than your partner whose friendships you value highly. As you recall each of these people, past and present, answer the question, "What about this person makes him or her a treasured friend?" Based on the characteristics that come to mind, write your own paragraph defining friendship.

What I want in a friend is . . .

Underline each friendship characteristic in the paragraph you just wrote. Circle any characteristic that is true or used to be true of your basic friendship with your partner.

WHAT I AM
AS A FRIEND

Friendship requires that two people make the effort together. Now that you've reminded yourself of what you value in specific friends, and in friendship generally, write a paragraph outlining your friendship qualities.

What I offer as a friend is . . .

MY PARTNER
AS A FRIEND

Now write another paragraph that describes your friendship with your partner at its very best.

What was great about my friendship with my partner was . . .

How many of the friendship characteristics you value in yourself or others exist in your relationship with your partner now? List each characteristic that still exists below.

If you were able to find some active ingredients of friendship in your current relationship, you have something to build on. If not, you at least have a clearer sense of what you've lost and what you're aiming for.

Personal Relationship Value #5—
PROMOTE YOUR PARTNER'S SELF-ESTEEM

There is a long-standing tradition in some cultures when naming a new baby that the child be given a name that is associated with a positive trait or value. The idea is that the family gives the child a positive sense of self into which to grow. When you promote your partner's self-esteem, you actively affirm every positive trait that does or could exist in him or her. You inspire your partner to operate at the highest level by showing that you believe in his or her worth and value.

THE HONOR ROLL

You are in a better position than anyone else in the world to know what is virtuous, honorable, and valuable in your partner. Perhaps you've forgotten many of those qualities during the pain and disappointment of your relationship. Maybe you have not observed them in action toward you for a long time. But the qualities exist, and you have the greatest power in your partner's life to reflect those qualities back to him or her day after day. What are the qualities in your partner that can be supported and nurtured? Loyalty? A sense of humor? High ideals? Persistence? Create a list of twenty qualities that characterize your partner. Then after each, write a specific instance in which you could have reinforced that quality by choosing to focus on that instead of some perceived flaw or failing.

1.

2.

3.

4.

5.

6.

7.

8.

9.

10.

11.

12.

13.

14.

15.

16.

17.

18.

19.

20.

Personal Relationship Value #6—
AIM YOUR FRUSTRATIONS IN THE RIGHT DIRECTION

You may be so used to the pileup of frustrations that you experience from day to day that you aren't even aware of the price you and your partner are paying. But you can be sure that frustrations find an outlet if you don't acknowledge and deal with them in a constructive way, and no one is more likely to be on the receiving end than your partner. You can change this pattern by paying attention and committing yourself to aiming your frustrations where they should be aimed—namely at their sources. The following exercise can start you on the road to greater awareness that will help repair the spirit with which you approach your partner in the future.

FRUSTRATION LOG

For one day to one week, accumulate a list of ten specific frustrations that you experience that are not related to your partner. You may have a self-image frustration. Or you may have one with another relationship. A frustration may come from your life at work or your time on the road. Whatever the frustrations are, record them below in the left-hand column. That's the easy part. What will be harder is to record with complete honesty how you would typically deal with the frustration. This exercise may help you better identify sources of your frustration, so you won't take it out on your partner. I want you to identify your own default behavior—what do you *usually* do when you get caught in a major traffic jam? When you weigh in much heavier than usual? When your friend keeps you waiting *again*? If need be, think back to a similar frustration in the recent past, and describe how you responded that time. Did you vent on the spot, stockpile the frustration, dump it on your partner later, or find a constructive response? Don't play coverup. You can't change what you don't acknowledge.

The problem is . . .	My response usually is . . .

Personal Relationship Value #7—

BE UP-FRONT AND FORTHRIGHT

Just as it is possible to vent emotions on your partner that he or she doesn't deserve, you can run into trouble when you refuse to be direct about something that is relevant to your partner. You will need first to be honest with yourself. How much of the emotion you feel toward your partner right now is a coverup for the real issues? The following exercises can help you look behind your surface emotions—anger, defensiveness, desire to judge, pouting—and locate the true issues and emotions that cause them. Only then will you be ready to be honest with your partner.

"I Put up
My Dukes
when . . ."

Check every statement that describes you at least some of the time in relation to your partner.

I feel anger when . . .

_____ my partner is having trouble at work

_____ my partner neglects to do something he or she promised to do

_____ I suspect that my partner is lying about something

_____ my partner refuses to take responsibility for wrongdoing

_____ my partner won't listen to or accept my point of view in a disagreement

_____ my partner is late or missing for an event that is especially important to me

_____ my partner puts down my family or friends

_____ my partner teases me about my appearance

_____ I need help and my partner is nowhere to be found

_____ my partner tells me what I'm doing wrong

_____ my partner hits me over the head with a list of problems the minute I walk in the door

_____ my partner does something foolish, and bad consequences occur

_____ my partner lets someone *else* down

_____ my partner treats our children (if you have them) unfairly

_____ my partner screws up our finances

_____ my partner doesn't tell me anything about his or her life away from me

_____ my partner doesn't include me in the things that he or she enjoys the most

_____ I need support and my partner gives me advice

_____ my partner explodes at me for no good reason

_____ my partner gives me the silent treatment

For each of the situations above that you marked with a check, change the "emotion word" that describes your reaction from *anger* to *fear, hurt,* or *frustration.* Then answer the relevant questions: "What specifically is it in this situation that I fear? Why? What makes it hurtful to me? Why? In what regard am I frustrated, and why?"

"I'D RATHER COVER UP BECAUSE . . ." As an additional way to look deeper within yourself for the sources of emotional dishonesty, write a paragraph describing what you think keeps you from expressing your emotions honestly to your partner. Write for five minutes without stopping (you will need to use a separate sheet of paper). Talk about what is at work in you when you cover up—emotionally, physically, verbally, mentally, or relationally.

Personal Relationship Value #8—
MAKE YOURSELF HAPPY RATHER THAN RIGHT

You may be right just about as often as you think you are. But how you express yourself and what you make of your rightness in relation to your partner will determine whether being right also makes you happy. Take a look at the areas where you may practice rightness at the expense of happiness. These will be areas that will require a new way of thinking and behaving if you hope to get your relationship back on solid ground.

YOUR
RIGHTEOUSNESS
QUOTIENT

Read the statements that follow. Some of them may apply to you, and some may not. But resist the temptation to say "never" when asked how often you need to be right in a disagreement with your partner. Give yourself 1 point for rarely, 2 for sometimes, 3 for regularly, 4 for almost always, and 5 for without fail—unless an item has absolutely nothing to do with your relationship.

	1	2	3	4	5
I insist that I'm right about how to drive safely.					
I insist that I'm right about raising kids.					
I insist that I'm right about good manners.					
I insist that I'm right about what "clean" means.					
I insist that I'm right about what should be considered a high priority.					
I insist that I'm right about who should take responsibility for what around the house.					
I insist that I'm right about the way we should use money.					
I insist that I'm right on matters of religion.					
I insist that I'm right in how we should treat extended family.					

	1	2	3	4	5
I insist that I'm right about how, when, and where we have sex.					
I insist that I'm right in conversations about politics.					
I insist that I'm right about how to furnish or decorate our home.					
I insist that I'm right about how to play sports.					
I insist that I'm right about what tastes good.					
I insist that I'm right about how to cook food on a grill.					
I insist that I'm right about what the neighbors will think.					
I insist that I'm right about how to handle problems.					

Scoring

If you scored between 17 and 33, you probably have a fairly balanced view of your judgment. You'll want to give your attention to more supportive ways of dealing with differences.

If you scored between 34 and 50, you're still ranking high on the "I need to win" scale.

If you scored between 51 and 67, you may be accurate in your assessment of how right you are, but you are far too willing to win at any cost.

If you scored between 68 and 85, you need to give a hard look not only at how you communicate but how realistic you are about being "in the know."

"JUST SUPPOSE ..." Choose one of the items that got the highest score from the preceding list. Now write a story about you and your partner discussing this issue in such a way that you both "win" by the time the discussion is over. Consider what parts such attitudes as understanding, compassion, tolerance, and empathy might play in the interaction you describe.

Personal Relationship Value #9—

ALLOW YOUR RELATIONSHIP TO TRANSCEND TURMOIL

Outrage happens. Maybe for you it's a weekly or even daily event. But as long as you allow your relationship to be held hostage to the tumult of the moment, you will add pressure and insecurity that will keep you from finding new and better ways to deal with the conflicts that inevitably surface in a relationship. Eliminate the threats to end your relationship, and you'll greatly enhance the potential of reconnection.

"OR ELSE!" Make a list of ten instances in your history with your partner when you acted, spoke, thought, or implied that your relationship was not worth the pain you were going through.

    1.

2.

3.

4.

5.

6.

7.

8.

9.

10.

Put a check mark beside each item on your list that you still believe is important enough to rank as a "deal-breaker" in your relationship. Then answer the following questions about any items
that you have checked. Be honest!

Did this break a promise that you and your partner made to each
other?

Did this betray the understanding of sexual exclusivity that you had established?

Did this jeopardize your physical safety or the safety of your children (if you have them)?

What would or did it take to allow you to forgive your partner?

Given a convincing reason to restore the relationship despite this item, would you?

Personal Relationship Value #10—

PUT MOTION INTO YOUR EMOTION

This is where the rubber hits the road. Wishing for something better doesn't make it happen. And regretting what is bad does not make the bad evaporate. You need to develop pro-active love behavior if you want to create change and inspire your partner to a higher standard. Don't let a lack of initiative or imagination rob you of something as precious and valuable as a solid, loving relationship.

LOVE ACTION

Begin now by exercising your thinking on the subject of loving behavior. List thirty different ways you can demonstrate that your relationship means enough to you that you are willing to put your best foot forward in it and for it.

1.

2.

3.

4.

5.

6.

7.

8.

9.

10.

11.

12.

13.

14.

15.

16.

17.

18.

19.

20.

21.

22.

23.

24.

25.

26.

27.

28.

29.

30.

ACTION
ASSIGNMENT

For the next week, put those great ideas you just listed to work. For the next seven days, answer the following questions.

	What did I do today that brought us closer together?	What did I do today that may have pushed us farther apart?
Day 1		
Day 2		
Day 3		
Day 4		
Day 5		
Day 6		
Day 7		

REPORT CARD   For each day that you filled in in the preceding chart, record in detail how the pro-active behavior felt, what difference it made, and whether (or how) your partner responded.

Day 1:

Day 2:

Day 3:

Day 4:

Day 5:

Day 6:

Day 7:

PERSONAL
RELATIONSHIP
VALUE
REMINDER

Make a copy of the ten Personal Relationship Values from this chapter on a card or paper that you can carry with you, post on the refrigerator door, stick to your bathroom mirror, or frame for your desk. Study them. Memorize them. Make them part of the way you think.

chapter 6

THE FORMULA FOR SUCCESS

Y ou have continued to lay a firm foundation for success. Now
you are ready to build some solid blocks of insight and understanding about your partner and your relationship that
will help you reconnect with your partner in a reality-based, meaningful way. Keep up the good work you've been doing. Trust me
when I tell you that it is adding up to your greatest potential for
success.

ARE YOU
READY?

Before you proceed, test your readiness. Only when you can honestly answer each of these statements with a "True" will you be
ready for the formula for success.

I realize that it's not too late.	**True**	**False**
It is reasonable for me to want a rewarding and fulfilling relationship.	**True**	**False**
I am entitled to, and deserve, a high-quality, caring relationship.	**True**	**False**
I have identified the wrong thinking that has previously contaminated my relationship.	**True**	**False**
I have identified the bad spirits that contaminated my relationship.	**True**	**False**

I have embraced the Personal Relationship Values that will configure me for success (see Chapter 5 in *Relationship Rescue*).	**True**	**False**
I have diagnosed and gotten real about the pain and problems in my relationship.	**True**	**False**
I accept and acknowledge full ownership of my contribution to where this relationship is.	**True**	**False**
I am committed to tapping into my core of consciousness.	**True**	**False**

If you answered "False" to any of the statements, ask yourself, "What do I need to do to change this 'False' into a 'True?' " Then do it!

WRITE YOUR
OWN
DEFINITIONS

At the heart of relationship success is a solid underlying friendship. Just to firm up your understanding of what I'm talking about, go back and reread pages 124 to 125 in *Relationship Rescue*. Then, based on what you've read, define the following terms, putting the definitions in your own words.

Friendship:

Needs:

Quality:

Job #1——MAKE YOUR NEEDS KNOWN—YOUR PERSONAL PROFILE

This is an exercise of self-discovery. As you enter it, commit yourself to do so with an open spirit and without self-judgment. Your needs are your needs. As you recognize and acknowledge them, you create a path toward having those needs met. So face yourself and your needs squarely and with courage.

EMOTIONAL
NEEDS

For every need that applies to you, put an X on the line to the left of it. But don't stop there. Expand on specific ways, times, and frequencies that further describe this need as you experience it. When you have worked your way through the existing list, adding your own details to each general item, continue in the provided space to add needs that occurred to you as you wrote. If you need more space, add paper of your own. Keep any added sheets with the workbook for later reference. Follow these directions for each of the categories of needs that follow.

_____ The need to feel, and be told, that I am loved

_____ The need to feel, and be told, that I am a valued, vital part of my partner's life

_____ The need to feel a sense of belonging to and with my partner

_____ The need to feel respected as an individual

_____ The need to feel needed for other than the tasks I perform

_____ The need to feel that I am a priority in my partner's life

_____ The need to feel special, above everyone else in my partner's life

_____ The need to feel that my partner is proud to call me his or her own

_____ The need to feel that I am trusted as a responsible partner

_____ The need to feel that my partner would choose me again

_____ The need to feel that I have been and can be forgiven for transgressions and flaws

_____ The need to feel accepted, flaws, fallacies, and all

_____ The need to feel that my partner and I are, above all else, close and trusted friends

_____ The need to feel desired

_____ The need to feel appreciated for who and what I am and do

_____ The need to feel passion between me and my relationship partner

PHYSICAL NEEDS

_____ The need to be touched and caressed

_____ The need to be kissed, even if casually

_____ The need to be hugged or held

_____ The need to feel that I am welcome in my partner's personal space

_____ The need to be physically welcomed when encountering my partner

_____ The need to feel that I am part of a couple when interacting with the world

_____ The need to feel encouraged and welcomed by nonverbal communications

_____ The need for tenderness

_____ The need for a satisfying and rewarding sexual life

SPIRITUAL NEEDS

_____ The need to feel that my personal spiritual values are supported without judgment

_____ The need to feel that my partner respects my spiritual needs

_____ The need to share a spiritual life, even if that spiritual life is experienced differently by me and my partner

_____ The need to know and feel that my individual beliefs and differences are respected, if not shared

SOCIAL NEEDS
_____ The need to be remembered with calls and acknowledgments when apart

_____ The need to feel that my partner will plan and structure his or her activities to include me

_____ The need to feel that social activities are shared rather than experienced individually

_____ The need for appropriate tenderness and support when in public

_____ The need to be encouraged and supported physically and emotionally when in public

_____ The need to hear sweet things in a social environment

_____ The need to be encouraged and supported in social situations

_____ The need to be treated with politeness and regard in social situations

_____ The need to share fun and joy in social situations

_____ The need to share a connection expressed through awareness and sensitivity by my partner

_____ The need to share joy and laughter

_____ The need to feel that I am the most important person in my partner's life and awareness when in a crowded, busy social environment

SECURITY NEEDS

_____ The need to know that my partner will stand by me in times of distress or conflict

_____ The need to feel that my partner will rally to my aid if needed

_____ The need to feel input and control with regard to the emotional aspects of the relationship

_____ The need to be supported by my partner

_____ The need to know that my partner is loyal and committed

_____ The need to know that our relationship will not be put at risk and hang in the balance because of any disagreements and confrontations

_____ The need to know that my partner is committed permanently

_____ The need to know that my partner is there for me in times of third-party conflicts and problems

_____ The need to know that my partner is my soft place to fall

IDENTIFYING FEARS

Remember that your fears may be masking, inhibiting, or confusing your needs and your ability to express them honestly to your partner. In the interest of building a deep and authentic understanding of what you bring to your relationship, you need to know and understand the fears that too often control you. Use the following list to stimulate your thinking about the fears that may bind you. As in the preceding exercise, mark each relevant fear with an

X. Then expand on it as it applies specifically to you and your life in the spaces that follow.

_____ The broad and sweeping fear of rejection

_____ The fear of inadequacy—physical, mental, emotional, sexual, social, or in any other category where I fear that I may not measure up

_____ The fear of abandonment

_____ The fear of disappointing or letting down my partner

Job #2—WORK TO DISCOVER THE NEEDS OF YOUR PARTNER—THE PARTNER PROFILE

As challenging as it may have been to verbalize a profile of yourself, it can't compare to the challenge, fun, and excitement of profiling your partner. However, be sure to stay alert to those two areas of danger: your fixed beliefs and your assumptions about who and what your partner is. This is a journey of investigation and discovery. Don't make the mistake of thinking that you already know your partner inside out. Instead, without judgmental attitudes and with an open mind, give your best, most objective attention to this fascinating enterprise.

PARTNER AWARENESS QUIZ

Answer the following questions as honestly as you can. Remember that you need to do this without consulting your partner. The point is to assess how aware of your partner you are now. Make this an honest appraisal.

I can name my partner's three best friends.	**True**	**False**
I know what accomplishments my partner is most proud of.	**True**	**False**
I can identify the happiest time in my partner's life.	**True**	**False**
I know what my partner considers to be his or her greatest losses in life.	**True**	**False**

I can describe what my partner considers to be his or her greatest area of difficulty in interacting with each of his parents.	**True**	**False**
I know what will be probably be playing on the radio when my partner is driving somewhere.	**True**	**False**
I can name the relatives that my partner would most likely try to avoid at a family reunion.	**True**	**False**
I can describe the most traumatic event that occurred in my partner's childhood.	**True**	**False**
My partner has clearly identified for me what he or she wants in life.	**True**	**False**
I can identify the obstacles that my partner believes are preventing his or her getting what he or she wants.	**True**	**False**
I know which of my partner's physical features he or she is least happy about.	**True**	**False**
I can recall the very first impressions I had of my partner.	**True**	**False**
I know what section of the Sunday newspaper my partner is likely to turn to first.	**True**	**False**
I can describe, in some detail, the home environment in which my partner was raised.	**True**	**False**
I know what makes my partner laugh.	**True**	**False**
I know what my partner's parents would probably say is the thing about my partner that they are most proud of.	**True**	**False**
I can describe two or three decisions my partner made before we met that my partner now regrets—and my partner can do the same about me.	**True**	**False**
I know which part of a restaurant menu my partner is likely to look at first.	**True**	**False**
I can quote three things my partner says to me that he or she says to no one else in this world.	**True**	**False**

I am thoroughly familiar with my partner's reli- **True   False**
gious beliefs.

Scoring
Give yourself 1 point for each true answer.
0 to 9   Miles to go, but the perfect opportunity on hand
10 or higher   Fairly accurate profile, but with much exploration
and discovery ahead

Now you're ready to move ahead into a detailed investigation.

FAMILY   Answer all the questions as fully and accurately as you can.
HISTORY

YOUR   How did your partner get his or her name?
PARTNER'S
FULL NAME

Is your partner named after someone?_____Who?_____
What is the significance of that person in your partner's life, or in
the lives of your partner's parents?

Is there any other special significance to your partner's name? Explain.

Does your partner like his or her name or not? Why?

AGE Does your partner consider his or her age an issue? In what way?

Does he or she feel too old? Too young?

Does your partner desire to be a different age? Explain.

Are your ages the same or different? Is that a problem?

MATERNAL RELATIONSHIP	Is your partner's mother living?	**Yes**	**No**
	If she is deceased, do you see any issue or problem there?	**Yes**	**No**
	Does your partner consider this relationship an asset rather than a liability?	**Yes**	**No**
	Do you consider your partner's relationship with his or her mother to be a healthy one?	**Yes**	**No**
	Does your partner feel that his or her mother is proud of him or her?	**Yes**	**No**
	Does your partner consistently treat this family member with dignity and respect?	**Yes**	**No**
	By contrast, would you say that your partner tends to take advantage of or exploit this family member?	**Yes**	**No**
	Is this relationship openly affectionate and warm?	**Yes**	**No**
	Is guilt a major part of the relationship?	**Yes**	**No**

WRITTEN EXERCISE   Please refer to the questions on pages 145 to 146 of *Relationship Rescue* to stimulate your thinking as you consider in writing the mechanics of your partner's relationship with his or her mother.

PATERNAL RELATIONSHIP	Is your partner's father living?	**Yes**	**No**
	If he is deceased, do you see any issue or problem there?	**Yes**	**No**
	Does your partner consider this relationship an asset rather than a liability?	**Yes**	**No**
	Do you consider your partner's relationship with his or her father to be a healthy one?	**Yes**	**No**
	Does your partner feel that his or her father is proud of him or her?	**Yes**	**No**
	Does your partner consistently treat this family member with dignity and respect?	**Yes**	**No**
	By contrast, would you say that your partner tends to take advantage of or exploit this family member?	**Yes**	**No**
	Is this relationship openly affectionate and warm?	**Yes**	**No**
	Is guilt a major part of the relationship?	**Yes**	**No**

WRITTEN EXERCISE

Please refer to the questions on pages 146 to 147 of *Relationship Rescue* to stimulate your thinking as you consider in writing the mechanics of your partner's relationship with his or her father.

SIBLING
RELATIONSHIP(S)

If your partner has more than one sibling, make photocopies of this page before you complete it. Make one copy per sibling to add to your workbook. You should complete this exercise for *each sibling*.

Is this sibling still living?	**Yes**	**No**
If he or she is deceased, do you see any issue or problem there?	**Yes**	**No**
Does your partner consider this relationship an asset rather than a liability?	**Yes**	**No**
Do you consider your partner's relationship with this brother or sister to be a healthy one?	**Yes**	**No**
Does your partner feel that this sibling is proud of him or her?	**Yes**	**No**
Does your partner consistently treat this family member with dignity and respect?	**Yes**	**No**
By contrast, would you say that your partner tends to take advantage of or exploit this family member?	**Yes**	**No**
Is this relationship openly affectionate and warm?	**Yes**	**No**
Is guilt a major part of the relationship?	**Yes**	**No**

WRITTEN
EXERCISE

Please refer to the questions on page 148 of *Relationship Rescue* to stimulate your thinking as you consider in writing the mechanics of your partner's relationship with his or her sibling(s).

RELATIONSHIP
SKETCH

Picture your partner's parents together: In your imagination, where are they? If you picture them indoors, what room are they in? What are they doing?

Is the relationship between them characterized by lots of affection, or is it more standoffish? How do they express affection for each other? Do they use particular physical gestures to communicate affection for each other? Do they have favorite expressions or pet phrases that they share with each other?

Now try to picture them caught up in a conflict. Do their disagreements frequently escalate into all-out war? Or do they treat any kind of conflict as embarrassing and unacceptable, such that even minor disagreements are quickly suppressed? How would you characterize their style of conflict? What strategies does each of them use for resolving the dispute? Perhaps each takes a stand, freely communicating his or her position. Maybe one of them quickly abandons the room, refusing to negotiate.

Have your partner's parents been faithful to each other?

Do they make each other laugh? How?

Are they friends with each other? Does each consider the other his or her best friend? If not, what need is left unfilled, such that he or she must turn outside the relationship to have that need met? By contrast, does each of them have a close-knit group of friends that he or she enjoys spending time with?

What kind of home environment have they created? Is there tension in the air? When visitors come calling, do those visitors immediately feel comfortable and welcome in the home? Or do they sit stiffly on the edges of their chairs, eager to escape?

What behavioral shortcomings or maladaptive behaviors do you see in your partner's parents? Maybe there are certain kinds of stresses or crises that one or both parents just can't handle very well. Think about those situations, and how the given parent is likely to react.

Now use what you have recorded above to prompt further insight into the relationship of your partner's parents to each other. Write about what you know of the connection between them.

YOUR
PARTNER'S
OTHER
RELATIONSHIPS

Who are your partner's best friends? Why are they his or her best friends? What is it about them that makes him or her want to spend time with them? How does he or she treat them?

Generally speaking, what is your partner's attitude toward the opposite sex?

Did your partner have best friends during childhood? Who were they?

What kinds of people does your partner not like?

How does your partner feel about and treat the elderly?

How does your partner feel about and treat animals?

Other than you, to whom does your partner turn for companionship and warmth?

Has your partner ever been betrayed? Has your partner ever had his or her heart broken? By whom? What were the circumstances? How did your partner respond?

What has been your partner's prior relationship history? What do you know about his or her relationships before the one in which you are now a part?

What kind of social life and pattern does your partner prefer? Do weekends and free evenings need to be filled with activity and new faces, or would your partner just as soon stay home? What's an ideal social occasion for your partner?

Does your partner have friends at work? What does he or she like about them?

Is your partner liked by his or her peers? Why or why not?

Does your partner seem to care what other people think about him or her?

Would you consider your partner to be a loyal person?

Is your partner faithful?

How does your partner feel about your family: your parents, siblings, and relatives?

Which people, or what kinds of people, intimidate your partner?

How does your partner feel about his or her station in life? Does your partner feel that he or she is way down in the pecking order, or is your partner proud of where he or she is?

How does your partner relate to authority?

YOUR PARTNER'S "ATTITUDE OF APPROACH"

Picture your partner and his or her way of being in the world. Then finish each of the statements that follow by circling the choice that most closely describes your partner.

1. When the two of us arrive at a cocktail party or similar event where strangers are present, my partner would rather
    a. *hover around the edges of the crowd, waiting for someone else to initiate a conversation*
    b. *head straight for the partygoers who seem to be having the most fun*
2. I would describe my partner as being
    a. *more participative*
    b. *more passive*
3. I would describe my partner as being
    a. *more of a leader*
    b. *more of a follower*
4. My partner
    a. *is a courageous person*
    b. *plays the game of life with sweaty palms*

5. Generally speaking, my partner can be described as
   a. *lazy*
   b. *industrious*
6. My partner is
   a. *mostly content and satisfied with his or her life*
   b. *restless and frustrated*
7. My partner
   a. *lives in a comfort zone, refusing to step out of familiar boundaries*
   b. *has an adventuresome spirit, and welcomes fresh challenges*
8. My partner tends to be
   a. *flexible*
   b. *rigid*

Now answer each of the following questions with a sentence or two that best relates to your partner.

What does your partner think is funny?

What does your partner find offensive?

Does your partner ever reminisce? If so, about what?

How does your partner feel about his or her childhood?

Would you say your partner finds it easy to express himself or herself emotionally?

How does your partner respond when the environment is emotionally charged?

YOUR PARTNER'S "FRUSTRATION SET" Now give some detailed thought to what your partner's greatest frustrations are. The following phrases and questions should help you zero in on the sources and strengths of the frustrations your partner deals with from day to day.

On the job

At home

Dealing with particular family members

Handling particular issues

Are there patterns to your partner's frustrations—that is, are there particular times and circumstances in which your partner is likely to feel especially upset?

Can you predict how your partner is likely to express his or her frustration? What does your partner do when frustrated?

Does your partner maintain a generally positive outlook, even when things aren't going well?

What does your partner do when angry?

Name three or four of your partner's pet peeves.

How important to your partner are peace and harmony?

Would you say your partner is forgiving or vindictive?

How competitive is your partner?

How does your partner feel about confrontation?

Is your partner a good sport? Is he or she a gracious winner?

Is your partner a whiner and a blamer, or does he or she generally accept what's done and seek to move on?

Does your partner have insecurities? What are they?

What does your partner do when hurt?

Does your partner feel appreciated?

Now, in a paragraph that draws on your answers to the questions you've just answered, describe two or three sources of frustration that may be present in different areas of your partner's life. Describe your partner's "frustration environment," including how he or she responds in the face of frustration.

SUCCESS,   Answer each of the following questions with a sentence or two.
FAILURE,
AND LOSS   How does your partner define success? Money? Absence of conflict?
             Peace at home? What does success consist of for your partner?

             What have been your partner's greatest successes in life? What
             have been his or her outstanding victories?

             What have been your partner's greatest failures? What have been
             his or her most challenging defeats?

What are your partner's limitations? Does he or she acknowledge them?

Have there been one or more major tragedies in your partner's life? What were they?

Can your partner apologize when wrong?

OCCUPATIONAL AND FINANCIAL CONCERNS

Answer each of the following questions with a sentence or two.

How satisfied with his or her work is your partner?

If your partner could choose a different job, what would it be? What satisfactions would that job provide that your partner does not currently get from his or her work?

How does your partner feel about his or her financial position in life?

Is your partner financially responsible?

MIND AND
BODY ISSUES

Answer each of the following questions with a sentence or two.

What is the parental legacy that your partner has inherited:

Medically?

Psychologically?

Relationally (having to do with effective relationships)?

How intelligent is your partner?

How intelligent does your partner think he or she is?

How does your partner feel about his or her own appearance?

What is your partner's favorite sport?

What is your partner's desired level of sexual activity?

What are your partner's favorite foods?

What kind of music does your partner like best?

What is your partner's favorite art?

What are your partner's interests?

What hobbies does your partner have?

PRINCIPLES AND PRIORITIES

Answer each of the following questions with a sentence or two.

Does your partner have and commit to principles? What are they? What beliefs does your partner have that rise to the level of conscious commitments?

Is there an area of your partner's life where he or she excels? What is it?

Is your partner especially committed to excellence in a particular area of his or her life?

What are your partner's political leanings?

What are your partner's top five priorities at this point in his or her life? List them.

1.

2.

3.

4.

5.

Is your partner optimistic about the future?

About what is your partner most passionate?

About what in his or her life is your partner most proud?

What are your partner's greatest fears?

What does your partner do when afraid?

What does your partner's spiritual life consist of?

What are your partner's spiritual or religious beliefs about life after death?

Time-out! Take a break. When you have regained some energy and are ready to focus fully and honestly on the following questions, answer them with the intention and assurance that you and you alone will see what you write.

FIRST QUESTION   If your partner could be anywhere he or she wanted to be

With anyone he or she wanted to be with

Doing anything he or she wanted to be doing . . .

What would it be?

SECOND
QUESTION
What was the happiest time in your partner's life?

If it was some time in the past, why did it end?

What happened to change the happiness your partner felt: Did he or she change, or did the world change?

THIRD
QUESTION
What does your partner want?

What are the obstacles to him or her having what he or she wants?

FOURTH
QUESTION
Why did your partner choose you for an intimate relationship? Knowing what you know of your partner's family history, relationship history, and overall makeup, what do you think were the major factors that attracted him or her to you and caused your partner to bring you into that private world?

FIFTH
QUESTION
What are your partner's major faults?

PUTTING IT
ALL
TOGETHER
Take some time before you move on to the next section to put together all the hard work you have done in this section. You may not have been able to answer all the questions completely. Perhaps there are some questions you couldn't answer at all. That's okay. Learning more about your partner and your relationship in the future will be part of the exciting process you've begun here. For now, you have accomplished a great deal, regardless of any gaps in your knowledge.

Review the entire personal profile you've just created, and allow that information to awaken your insight into your partner's point of view. Then create a list that describes your partner under each of the need categories that follow.

Emotional Needs

Physical Needs

Spiritual Needs

Social Needs

Security Needs

For *each need* that you listed in the five categories, go back and answer this question: "What are three things I can do, right now and consistently in the future, to fill the need that my partner has in this area?"

chapter 7

RECONNECTING WITH YOUR PARTNER

Y ou are about to embark on the most exciting part of the reconnection process so far. You have worked hard to know and reconnect with yourself. You've also done a lot of preliminary work diagnosing, investigating, describing, and understanding your partner and your relationship as it is right now. As you prepare to begin a meaningful dialogue with your partner, keep in mind the essential maxim that only a win/win situation will meet the needs of both of you in such a way that you can work productively toward a better relationship.

NEGOTIATOR'S
TUTORIAL

Here's a checklist of some important attitudes and approaches that will help you create the win/win situation you want. (You may want to reread the chart on page 178 in *Relationship Rescue*.) Fill in the spaces as you go.

The dialogue is not *for* me or *against* my partner—it's on behalf of the two of us. I can be on the lookout for and constantly express shared benefits. Some examples of mutual benefit are:

The dialogue is not about someone being stronger and someone being weaker. Our *relationship* is troubled and needs to be strengthened. I will keep that center stage. I can express this by avoiding such accusations as:

My partner does not need to "deserve" the effort *I* am about to invest. *I* deserve it, and *our relationship* deserves it. I will take the respect I have for myself and our relationship and exercise it toward my partner. Some simple ways I can demonstrate the respect I hope to be shown myself are:

I will continue to be aware of my partner's needs for acceptance, self-respect, and security and seek to serve those needs in the midst of the honest dialogue ahead. For example, these statements included in the dialogue would help to meet such needs:

I will continue to be aware of my partner's need for validation and take care that I share the work I've done so far in as affirming and encouraging a manner as possible. I can, for instance, frame what I say in such ways as these:

I am 100 percent accountable for my life, so I will take responsibility for bringing a win/win spirit to the table day after day. I can show my optimism by:

Because this is all about winning for our relationship, I will not seek or be satisfied with any solution or dialogue that is less than a success for both of us. By *success*, I mean:

Understanding my partner is as important to the process as being understood by my partner. I will consciously lay aside set beliefs and assumptions and listen as though I'm finding things out from my partner for the first time. Some negative attitudes I need to put aside in order to really listen are:

In order to avoid falling into old, unhappy patterns as we talk, I need to keep the ultimate goal of a better, happier relationship before us at all times. If my partner takes the dialogue in former directions, here are some statements I can use to keep myself on track:

I will continue to do the preparation work of "facilitator" as we work through this process of reconnection, remembering the needs of my partner, as well as my own, and exercising the qualities of a negotiator. I see these qualities as (please reread pages 166 to 179 in *Relationship Rescue* to remind yourself of the negotiation attitudes):

STEP 1:
OPEN THE
RECONNECTION
DIALOGUE

You now enter into the dialogue itself. This section of the workbook is designed with two purposes in mind. First, it offers you guidance and space to prepare in writing for each step. Second, it provides you with space for a written debrief. I can't emphasize enough how valuable both of these exercises will be in absorbing and assessing the ongoing dialogue. Be sure to use this tool candidly and faithfully. Reread pages 166 to 169 in *Relationship Rescue*, review pages 193 to 196 in the workbook, and then proceed.

"MY OPENING STATEMENT"   I intend to begin by saying:

I see these immediate and meaningful benefits to my partner:

If my partner responds in a negative fashion, I can say:

DEBRIEF   Use this space to record and assess what happened when enacting Step 1, what followed between you and your partner, and how you feel about it.

With your experience in mind, revisit the "Negotiator's Tutorial," and note any qualities of attitude or approach that you need to strengthen for the next step.

STEP 2:
DESCRIBE THE
WORK YOU
HAVE BEEN
DOING

At this point, you will present what you have done so far. Reread pages 169 to 171 of *Relationship Rescue*, review pages 193 to 196 in the workbook, and proceed.

TALKING
POINTS

On page 170 of *Relationship Rescue*, I identify numerous talking points that are crucial to this step in reconnecting. Extract the points from the book, and put them in your own words here, being as specific and personal as possible as you interpret them for your own use in dialogue with your partner.

DEBRIEF

Use this space to record and assess what happened when enacting Step 2, what followed between you and your partner, and how you feel about it.

With your experience in mind, revisit the "Negotiator's Tutorial," and note any qualities of attitude or approach that you need to strengthen for the next step.

STEP 3:
DESCRIBE
YOUR EFFORTS
TO GET BACK
TO YOUR
CORE OF
CONSCIOUSNESS

Reread pages 2 to 3 and 171 in *Relationship Rescue*, review pages 193 to 196 in the workbook, and proceed.

"WHO I
COULD BE"

My understanding of the "core of consciousness," in my own words, is . . .

Some key qualities I have rediscovered in myself that I would like to communicate to my partner are . . .

DEBRIEF

Use this space to record and assess what happened when enacting Step 3, what followed between you and your partner, and how you feel about it.

With your experience in mind, revisit the "Negotiator's Tutorial," and note any qualities of attitude or approach that you need to strengthen for the next step.

STEP 4:
TALK ABOUT
THE TEN
RELATIONSHIP
MYTHS

Reread pages 40 to 63 and 171 to 172 in *Relationship Rescue*, review pages 193 to 196 in the workbook, and proceed.

TEN MYTHS

Create an abbreviated list of the ten myths, and describe them in your own words.

1.

2.

3.

4.

5.

6.

7.

8.

9.

10.

DEBRIEF Use this space to record and assess what happened when enacting Step 4, what followed between you and your partner, and how you feel about it.

With your experience in mind, revisit the "Negotiator's Tutorial," and note any qualities of attitude or approach that you need to strengthen for the next step.

STEP 5: Reread pages 66 to 93 and 172 to 173 in *Relationship Rescue*,
EXPLAIN THE review pages 193 to 196 in the workbook, and proceed.
BAD SPIRIT

TEN Create your own abbreviated list of the ten characteristics of a bad
CHARACTERISTICS spirit, with a short description of each.

1.

2.

3.

4.

5.

Record your thoughts about the character you would have in mind if you took another chance. Then write about how you will respond to your opponent the next time you decide to take a chance.

6.

7.

8.

9.

10.

Record your choice of a specific characteristic you have identified in yourself, and rehearse here, in writing, how you will present to your partner the incident or occasion that illustrates it.

DEBRIEF   Use this space to record and assess what happened when enacting Step 5, what followed between you and your partner, and how you feel about it.

With your experience in mind, revisit the "Negotiator's Tutorial," and note any qualities of attitude or approach that you need to strengthen for the next step.

STEP 6:   Reread pages 96 to 122 and 173 to 174 of the *Relationship Rescue*, INTRODUCE   review pages 193 to 196 of the workbook, and proceed.
THE
PERSONAL
RELATIONSHIP
VALUES

PERSONAL   Create an abbreviated list of the ten personal relationship values, RELATIONSHIP   and after each, describe it as you will to your partner. For *at least* VALUES   *one value*, identify a particular instance in which you saw it at work between you and your partner. If you can find a specific, personal example of more than one, that's even better.

1.

2.

3.

4.

5.

6.

7.

8.

9.

10.

DEBRIEF   Use this space to record and assess what happened when enacting Step 6, what followed between you and your partner, and how you feel about it.

With your experience in mind, revisit the "Negotiator's Tutorial," and note any qualities of attitude or approach that you need to strengthen for the next step.

STEP 7: SHARE THE FORMULA FOR SUCCESS IN A RELATIONSHIP

Reread pages 123 to 126 and 174 to 175 in *Relationship Rescue*, review pages 193 to 196 in the workbook, and proceed.

"IN MY OWN WORDS"

As I understand it and intend to communicate it to my partner, the formula for success in a relationship is . . .

DEBRIEF

Use this space to record and assess what happened when enacting Step 7, what followed between you and your partner, and how you feel about it.

With your experience in mind, revisit the "Negotiator's Tutorial," and note any qualities of attitude or approach that you need to strengthen for the next step.

STEP 8: SHARE YOUR PARTNER PROFILE
Reread pages 175 to 176 in *Relationship Rescue*, review pages 193 to 196 in the workbook, and proceed.

"MY OPENING STATEMENT"
This is crucial! Take the time to prepare how you will introduce this aspect of your work in the most sensitive and affirming way possible. Remember that your partner could easily feel threatened or defensive at this stage. Your job is to be the consummate diplomat.

DEBRIEF
Use this space to record and assess what happened when enacting Step 8, what followed between you and your partner, and how you feel about It.

With your experience in mind, revisit the "Negotiator's Tutorial," and note any qualities of attitude or approach that you need to strengthen for the next step.

STEP 9:
CLARIFY YOUR
PARTNER'S
NEEDS

Reread pages 176 to 177 in *Relationship Rescue*, review pages 193 to 196 in the workbook, and proceed.

DIPLOMACY
PRACTICE

List at least ten needs that you believe you have identified in your partner. After each, write out your plan for how to communicate your understanding of that need in the most diplomatic and validating manner possible.

1.

2.

3.

4.

5.

6.

7.

8.

9.

10.

DEBRIEF Use this space to record and assess what happened when enacting
Step 9, what followed between you and your partner, and how you
feel about it.

With your experience in mind, revisit the "Negotiator's Tutorial," and note any qualities of attitude or approach that you need to strengthen for the next step.

STEP 10:
SHARING
YOUR OWN
PERSONAL
PROFILE

Reread pages 177 to 178 in *Relationship Rescue*, review pages 193 to 196 in the workbook, and proceed.

THE POT OF
GOLD

You are taking the risk of personal vulnerability with your partner at this point. Why? Remind yourself by recording here ten great reasons for opening yourself to your partner in this way.

1.

2.

3.

4.

5.

6.

7.

8.

9.

10.

DEBRIEF   Use this space to record and assess what happened when enacting Step 10, what followed between you and your partner, and how you feel about it.

With your experience in mind, revisit the "Negotiator's Tutorial," and note any qualities of attitude or approach that you need to strengthen for the next step.

THE NEXT STEP   The ten steps you have just completed are only the beginning of a lifelong process. Now you will move into the programming and action phases of the reconnection process. Exercise your commitment here and now in writing. With your partner, set a date to begin the fourteen days of loving with honesty. Include details on how, when, where, and why you are both agreeing to this essential process.

I have agreed with my partner to begin the fourteen days of loving with honesty on _____.

How:

At this time of day:

In this setting:

Because:

chapter 8

FOURTEEN DAYS OF LOVING
WITH HONESTY

Now you build not only for immediate changes of attitude and action, but for lasting success. And you do this by committing yourselves to time with each other that will begin to build the values, attitudes, behaviors, and understanding that are vital to a successful long-term relationship. This section of the workbook is designed to give you a daily checklist of each day's assignments, as well as journal space for your five minutes' minimum of writing following the day's activities.

WHAT I FEAR MOST IN THIS PROCESS

Reread pages 180 to 183 in *Relationship Rescue* before going any further. Then finish the sentences that follow.

What I fear most in this process is . . .

WHAT I MOST   What I most hope for in this process is . . .
HOPE FOR IN
THIS PROCESS

Remember: If your partner refuses to participate, you owe it to yourself and your relationship to proceed on your own!

DAY 1   Reread pages 183 to 188 in *Relationship Rescue*.

MORNING   The affirmation action I chose for today was:

It resulted in:

meeting one of the needs of my partner (describe the need and how you met it)

relieving tension (explain in what way)

introducing something positive into our relationship (describe)

Record on a card:

1. Your Core of Consciousness
2. The Ten Myths about Relationships
3. The Ten Characteristics of Bad Spirit
4. The Ten Personal Relationship Values.

JOURNAL FOR DAY 1

Topic 1: I chose you because . . .

Topic 2: My greatest fear has been . . .

Topic 3: What I hope to gain is . . .

DAY 2   Reread pages 188 to 189 in *Relationship Rescue*.

MORNING   The affirmation action I chose for today was:

It resulted in:

meeting one of the needs of my partner (describe the need and how you met it)

relieving tension (explain in what way)

introducing something positive into our relationship (describe)

JOURNAL FOR
DAY 2

Topic 1: My greatest contributions to this relationship are . . .

Topic 2: I have contaminated this relationship by . . .

Topic 3: I am most excited about our future because . . .

DAY 3   Reread pages 189 to 191 in *Relationship Rescue*.

MORNING   The affirmation action I chose for today was:

It resulted in:

meeting one of the needs of my partner (describe the need and
how you met it)

relieving tension (explain in what way)

introducing something positive into our relationship (describe)

JOURNAL FOR
DAY 3

Topic 1: The negatives that I took away from my mother and father's relationship were . . .

Topic 2: The most positive things that I took from my mother and father's relationship were . . .

Topic 3: Our relationship has such a better chance because . . .

DAY 4   Reread pages 191 to 192 in *Relationship Rescue*.

MORNING   The affirmation action I chose for today was:

It resulted in:

meeting one of the needs of my partner (describe the need and how you met it)

relieving tension (explain in what way)

introducing something positive into our relationship (describe)

JOURNAL FOR
DAY 4

Topic 1: You should love and cherish me because . . .

Topic 2: If I lost you, it would hurt me because . . .

Topic 3: My sincere dreams for our relationship are . . .

DAY 5   Reread pages 192 to 194 in *Relationship Rescue*.

MORNING   The affirmation action I chose for today was:

It resulted in:

meeting one of the needs of my partner (describe the need and
how you met it)

relieving tension (explain in what way)

introducing something positive into our relationship (describe)

JOURNAL FOR DAY 5

Topic 1: Agreements that I have made with you and then broken or failed to live up to are . . .

Topic 2: It hurts me when you break agreements because . . .

Topic 3: I feel better about myself when I treat you with dignity and respect because . . .

DAY 6   Reread pages 194 to 195 in *Relationship Rescue*.

MORNING   The affirmation action I chose for today was:

It resulted in:

meeting one of the needs of my partner (describe the need and how you met it)

relieving tension (explain in what way)

introducing something positive into our relationship (describe)

JOURNAL FOR
DAY 6

Topic 1: Forgiveness and acceptance instead of judgment toward you help me because . . .

Topic 2: Forgiveness and acceptance instead of judgment toward myself help me because . . .

Topic 3: I want and need your forgiveness because . . .

DAY 7

Reread pages 196 to 197 in *Relationship Rescue*.

MORNING

The affirmation action I chose for today was:

It resulted in:

meeting one of the needs of my partner (describe the need and how you met it)

relieving tension (explain in what way)

introducing something positive into our relationship (describe)

JOURNAL FOR DAY 7

Topic 1: The things that are going well for me in my life are . . .

Topic 2: The things that are not going well for me in my life are . . .

Topic 3: The excuses I would typically make if our relationship does not turn out well are . . .

DAY 8   Reread pages 197 to 198 in *Relationship Rescue*.

MORNING   The affirmation action I chose for today was:

It resulted in:

meeting one of the needs of my partner (describe the need and how you met it)

relieving tension (explain in what way)

introducing something positive into our relationship (describe)

JOURNAL FOR
DAY 8

Topic 1: Our greatest barriers to a successful relationship have been . . .

Topic 2: Our greatest assets in having a successful relationship are . . .

Topic 3: Our relationship is worth all of our hard work because . . .

DAY 9   Reread pages 198 to 200 in *Relationship Rescue*.

MORNING   The affirmation action I chose for today was:

It resulted in:

meeting one of the needs of my partner (describe the need and how you met it)

relieving tension (explain in what way)

introducing something positive into our relationship (describe)

JOURNAL FOR
DAY 9

Topic 1: My "tapes" or fixed beliefs about men are . . .

Topic 2: My "tapes" or fixed beliefs about women are . . .

Topic 3: My "tapes" or fixed beliefs about relationships are . . .

DAY 10   Reread pages 200 to 201 in *Relationship Rescue*.

MORNING   The affirmation action I chose for today was:

It resulted in:

meeting one of the needs of my partner (describe the need and how you met it)

relieving tension (explain in what way)

introducing something positive into our relationship (describe)

JOURNAL FOR DAY 10

Topic 1: What I like least about me is . . .

Topic 2: What I like most about me is . . .

Topic 3: What I like least about you is . . .

Topic 4: What I like most about you is . . .

DAY 11   Reread pages 201 to 203 in *Relationship Rescue*.

MORNING   The affirmation action I chose for today was:

It resulted in:

meeting one of the needs of my partner (describe the need and how you met it)

relieving tension (explain in what way)

introducing something positive into our relationship (describe)

JOURNAL FOR   Topic 1: The category that best fits me is _____
DAY 11   because . . .

Topic 2: The category that best fits you is _____ because . . .

Topic 3: I can best use my category to contribute to our relationship by . . .

Topic 4: I could possibly contaminate our relationship if I allowed my defining characteristics to . . .

DAY 12   Reread pages 204 to 205 in *Relationship Rescue.*

MORNING   The affirmation action I chose for today was:

It resulted in:

meeting one of the needs of my partner (describe the need and how you met it)

relieving tension (explain in what way)

introducing something positive into our relationship (describe)

JOURNAL FOR   Topic 1: The greatest pain I have experienced was . . .
DAY 12

Topic 2: The worst loneliness I have experienced was . . .

Topic 3: I have never felt more loved and valued than when . . .

DAY 13   Reread pages 205 to 206 in *Relationship Rescue*.

MORNING   The affirmation action I chose for today was:

It resulted in:

meeting one of the needs of my partner (describe the need and how you met it)

relieving tension (explain in what way)

introducing something positive into our relationship (describe)

JOURNAL FOR DAY 13
Topic 1: If I had the power to change your experiences of life in any way, I would . . .

Topic 2: I am most proud of you when . . .

Topic 3: I want you to feel really special because . . .

DAY 14   Reread pages 206 to 208 in *Relationship Rescue*.

MORNING   The affirmation action I chose for today was:

It resulted in:

meeting one of the needs of my partner (describe the need and how you met it)

relieving tension (explain in what way)

introducing something positive into our relationship (describe)

JOURNAL FOR
DAY 14

Topic 1: I think you are the most sexy and sensual when you . . .

Topic 2: You make me feel sexy and sensual when you . . .

Topic 3: The gifts I see in you are . . .

YOUR
MISSION
STATEMENT

Your final assignment grows out of a completed fourteen days in which you carried out every one of the "Loving with Honesty" assignments. Ideally, you completed the assignments jointly with your partner. If so, use the space provided here to record privately the life decision that you and your partner have affirmed together in a mission statement. If you completed the assignments alone, then use this space to create your own mission statement concerning the ongoing work you will do to inspire your partner's participation in the future.

part iv

AIM FOR THE BEST

Before you begin this portion of the *Relationship Rescue Workbook*, read or reread Chapters 9 and 10 and the conclusion of *Relationship Rescue*.

I'm proud of you for coming this far in a challenging and probably scary process that many people will never even try. I'm proud of you for taking a stand for yourself and your relationship, recognizing its importance, and giving it its due. But I can't set you loose until I've made sure you understand that good intentions, new insights, and even all the work you've done so far won't give you what you want. *If you want different, you have to do different.* Not just for now, while your enthusiasm is at a peak and your energy is high, but for a lifetime. You have to build a way of life that supports what you want on every side. You and your partner have to undo a load of programming and create a *new* program. You need to reach past this initial stage of momentum and optimism into the long term. These final exercises are designed to give you the tools to manage your relationship. Take them, learn them, and put them to use. If you do, I promise you rewards now and for the life of your relationship.

chapter 9

RED ALERT — RELATIONSHIPS ARE
MANAGED, NOT CURED

I'm banking on the expectation that you won't quit until you've gone the distance. If you stop short now, you'll throw away all the hard work you've done so far. If you keep going and learn the basics of managing your relationship, you'll build a solid structure on a firm foundation and keep the momentum going in the direction of a better relationship. Treat the following exercises with all the seriousness and determination that you've given to the rest. You'll be glad that you did.

PRIORITY MANAGEMENT

Let's keep one thing straight. The quality of your relationship has to be a top priority in your life, or it's going to fall right back into its old, destructive, unhappy patterns. Making your relationship a top priority means making its health and vitality the basis on which you build your entire life. Every thought, behavior, and emotion is put to this test: "Does this support my priority of maintaining the relationship?" When the answer is no, stop and turn until you're headed in the right direction again.

"OUT WITH THE OLD"

Make a list of twenty-five specific ways that you have entertained thoughts, behaviors, or emotions in the past that sidelined your relationship—in other words, did not support the high-priority status you are now going to give your relationship. You've done enough background work by now that this assignment should come easily. Do as much reviewing as you need to do. Be forthright and honest. Concentrate on the real culprits in your attitudes. Don't let yourself off the hook. This is an important opportunity to remind yourself of the programming that you're leaving behind.

1.

2.

3.

4.

5.

6.

7.

8.

9.

10.

11.

12.

13.

14.

15.

16.

17.

18.

19.

20.

21.

22.

23.

24.

25.

"IN WITH THE NEW" Now, in addition to the list you just completed, use the positive work you accomplished in the "Fourteen Days of Loving with Honesty" to create a list of twenty-five specific ways that you can use thoughts, behaviors, and emotions to give the highest level of priority to your relationship. Think in terms of time, attitudes, and belief system.

1.

2.

3.

4.

5.

6.

7.

8.

9.

10.

11.

12.

13.

14.

15.

16.

17.

18.

19.

20.

21.

22.

23.

24.

25.

PRIORITY
PLAN

Now translate the two lists into a written paragraph. Describe the *how*, *what*, *when*, *why*, and *who* of the changes needed to put and keep your relationship in first place in your life. (You will need to use a separate piece of paper for this.)

BEHAVIOR
MANAGEMENT

Priority management has to do with the importance you give your relationship. Behavior management has to do with behaving your way to happiness. Simply stated, this means behaving in ways that define what *happy* means to you in the context of your relationship. I want you to look forward and see in your mind and heart the happy relationship you want. Then I want you to start building the history that supports it.

"WHO I WANT TO BE"

Remember this formula: Be—Do—Have. At the start of this process, you worked to reconnect to your core of consciousness. Recall that core in writing here. Describe yourself in terms of at least ten positive statements that reflect your values, beliefs, strengths, and talents. You should be able to do this with new depth as a result of the intensive work you've done.

I am . . .

1.

2.

3.

4.

5.

6.

7.

8.

9.

10.

Now write a summary paragraph about the "real you" here.

"THAT MEANS
I WILL . . ."   You've just described the "Be" part of the formula. Now get real about the "Do" part. Specify at least twenty ways of acting out "Who I Want to Be" in relation to your partner.

I will . . .

1.

2.

3.

4.

5.

6.

7.

8.

9.

10.

11.

12.

13.

14.

15.

16.

17.

18.

19.

20.

GOALS
MANAGEMENT

Making your relationship a top priority and managing your behavior in relation to what you want the relationship to be are crucial steps toward maintaining your focus and momentum. But you also need a particular plan to deal with both the weaknesses that have short-circuited your relationship in the past and the strengths that you have identified. Your plan can be understood in terms of setting goals. Become an active goal-setter, and you'll go a long way toward keeping your relationship on a forward path.

"OUR GREATEST STRENGTHS AS A COUPLE" Your strengths as a couple are powerful building blocks. Identify ten relationship strengths you and your partner have. Be specific as you describe what you see as the most valuable parts of your life together. Then create goals for each to make sure that you enhance those aspects of your life and increase their frequency in your shared experience. I've given you a place to break each goal down into behaviors and observable elements. If you need reminding as to how this works, reread pages 217 to 219 in *Relationship Rescue*.

Strength #1

Goals	Schedule	Interval Steps	Accountability Plan	Outcome Criteria

Strength #2

Goals	Schedule	Interval Steps	Accountability Plan	Outcome Criteria

Strength #3

Goals	Schedule	Interval Steps	Accountability Plan	Outcome Criteria

Strength #4

Goals	Schedule	Interval Steps	Accountability Plan	Outcome Criteria

Strength #5

Goals	Schedule	Interval Steps	Accountability Plan	Outcome Criteria

Strength #6

Goals	Schedule	Interval Steps	Accountability Plan	Outcome Criteria

Strength #7

Goals	Schedule	Interval Steps	Accountability Plan	Outcome Criteria

Strength #8

Goals	Schedule	Interval Steps	Accountability Plan	Outcome Criteria

Strength #9

Goals	Schedule	Interval Steps	Accountability Plan	Outcome Criteria

Strength #10

Goals	Schedule	Interval Steps	Accountability Plan	Outcome Criteria

"OUR WORST WEAKNESSES AS A COUPLE"

Just as you recognize that you have strengths as a couple and plan to build on those strengths, you have to acknowledge that you have weaknesses as a couple and put a "goals plan" in place to overcome them. In this way, you can turn the realities of weaknesses into positive changes in your relationship. As you did for the strengths, name ten of the most prominent weaknesses that you've uncovered in the work you've been doing. Then set your goals for change and fill in the details that will make them happen.

Weakness #1

Goals	Schedule	Interval Steps	Accountability Plan	Outcome Criteria

Weakness #2

Goals	Schedule	Interval Steps	Accountability Plan	Outcome Criteria

Weakness #3

Goals	Schedule	Interval Steps	Accountability Plan	Outcome Criteria

Weakness #4

Goals	Schedule	Interval Steps	Accountability Plan	Outcome Criteria

Weakness #5

Goals	Schedule	Interval Steps	Accountability Plan	Outcome Criteria

Weakness #6

Goals	Schedule	Interval Steps	Accountability Plan	Outcome Criteria

Weakness #7

Goals	Schedule	Interval Steps	Accountability Plan	Outcome Criteria

Weakness #8

Goals	Schedule	Interval Steps	Accountability Plan	Outcome Criteria

Weakness #9

Goals	Schedule	Interval Steps	Accountability Plan	Outcome Criteria

Weakness #10

Goals	Schedule	Interval Steps	Accountability Plan	Outcome Criteria

DIFFERENCE
MANAGEMENT

I'm sure after reading *Relationship Rescue* and working through this workbook, you've begun to wake up to the fact that you have sometimes judged your partner or been judged by your partner for the simple reason that you are different from each other. Your differences are generally not good or bad, but rather neutral differences. Managing those differences becomes key to a happy relationship and demands that you put the ten Personal Relationship Values to work in your relationship. It's time to start valuing your differences for the ways that they can complement one another. Be prepared for the conflicts that your personal history has already taught you can arise. And make a habit of remembering that you are two separate people who legitimately have individual points of view, belief systems, and personality traits. That's not just okay— it's great!

DIFFERENCE
CHECKLIST

Here's a quickie exercise that may help you to put your differences into a perspective that supports the top-priority status you have given your relationship. These are only some of many traits that characterize a person as an individual. But these and other traits multiply the differences between two people by creating differing points of view on a wide range of subjects. You may want to make your own list *with* your partner, as well. Mark the appropriate box or boxes to the right of each characteristic. You will begin to see how differences in these traits or descriptions—all of which are morally neutral—can add up between two individuals to cause some tension.

Characteristic	Me	You	Neither	Both
Intelligent				
Morning person				
Emotional				
Night owl				

Characteristic	Me	You	Neither	Both
Insightful				
Physically strong				
Decisive				
Logical				
Sensitive				
Good with money				
Intuitive				
Verbally expressive				
Physically expressive				
Assertive				
Diplomatic				
Sensible				
Handy with tools				
Self-disciplined				
In tune with nature				
Mechanically inclined				
Artistic				
Funny				
Inventive				
Shrewd				
Extroverted				

Characteristic	Me	You	Neither	Both
Introverted				
Discerning				
Good with children				
Good in social situations				
Imaginative				

MEDITATIONS ON DIFFERENCES

Now that you've given some fresh thought to the many ways in which you and your partner remain individuals in the midst of your partnership, spend some time thinking about the positive effects that your separate identities have on your relationship. Answer each of the questions that follow with at least a paragraph.

What do I gain personally because we're different?

What does our relationship gain because we're different?

What would I lose if we had no differences? What would we lose?

ADMIRATION
MANAGEMENT

You have already given some thought to the value that the differences between you and your partner add to you and your relationship. Now I want you to extend that thinking to a daily practice of appreciating your partner. I want you to make a habit of noticing what is admirable in your partner, not for what it gives you, but for its own sake. I want you to become your partner's number-one fan.

"I ADMIRE
YOU"

For the next two weeks—fourteen days—keep an ongoing list of things you admire about your partner. On Day 1, I want you to record at least five qualities, characteristics, actions, habits, or attitudes that you observe and admire about your partner. Add at least two items a day as you complete the two-week log.

Day 1:

Day 2:

Day 3:

Day 4:

Day 5:

Day 6:

Day 7:

Day 8:

Day 9:

Day 10:

Day 11:

Day 12:

Day 13:

Day 14:

"I ADMIRE ME, TOO"   As you focus on your partner's many positive traits and characteristics, take another positive look at yourself. Keep a log of what you see in yourself, as well. In this case, I want you to notice the ways that you are acting on the basis of your core of consciousness. Go back and review the early chapters of *Relationship Rescue* and the beginning of this workbook to get you going. As you did for your partner, list at least five qualities on Day 1, and at least two more for every day of the remaining two weeks.

Day 1:

Day 2:

Day 3:

Day 4:

Day 5:

Day 6:

Day 7:

Day 8:

Day 9:

Day 10:

Day 11:

Day 12:

Day 13:

Day 14:

LETTER OF
RECOMMENDATION

As a way of wrapping up what you have observed and admired, write a letter of recommendation on behalf of your partner. Write it as though you were recommending your partner to a third party. As with any letter of recommendation, take care to describe your partner truly and positively, seeking to show him or her in the best light while being honest and realistic.

chapter 10

THE DOCTOR IS "IN"

I wish that I could speak with each reader face to face. *Relationship Rescue: A Seven-Step Strategy for Reconnecting with Your Partner* and this workbook are my effort to come as close to a personal conversation with you as possible. If you have read the book and fulfilled the assignments in this workbook, you have the information, insight, and tools to face your relationship problems and create something better. Take time now to consider those issues that are at the top of your trouble list in light of all you've learned.

"WHAT'S THE PROBLEM?" I'm sure that over the course of the weeks or months of this study, specific questions have occurred to you. These have to do with the particular people you and your partner are, the specific history you each bring to your relationship, and the history you've created together. Zero in right now on the ten most compelling questions that have come up. Record them here.

1.

2.

3.

4.

5.

6.

7.

8.

9.

10.

Now go back to the questions and answers I've provided for you in Chapter 10 of *Relationship Rescue*. After each of the ten questions you identified in the previous exercise, record which of my example questions provide some insight or information that is relevant. Then extract the answer and advice that relates to each question and write the pertinent material out beneath the question. Use these questions and the information from me for ongoing conversations between you and your partner. Structure your conversations in the same way you structured your "Fourteen Days of Loving with Honesty." As you discuss your specific questions, you will probably find that you both begin to see new aspects of *Relationship Rescue* that are relevant.

CHECKLIST
FOR CHANGE

Based on your questions and discussions, create a checklist with your partner of the five most important issues you need to keep working on together.

1.

2.

3.

4.

5.

PROGRAMMING
IMPROVEMENT

As a further step toward reprogramming your relationship, turn to the seven rules of engagement on pages 233 to 237 of *Relationship Rescue*. In the space that follows, let each of the rules speak to you through your own experience. Begin by writing a paragraph that describes specific ways in which you and your partner have broken each rule in your relationship. Follow your description with three specific ways that *you* can apply the rule in the future.

Rule One: Take it private and keep it private.

We've broken this rule by . . .

We can apply this rule by . . .

1.

2.

3.

Rule Two: Keep it relevant.

We've broken this rule by . . .

We can apply this rule by . . .

   1.

   2.

   3.

Rule Three: Keep it real.

We've broken this rule by . . .

We can apply this rule by . . .

    1.

    2.

    3.

Rule Four: Avoid character assassination.

We've broken this rule by . . .

We can apply this rule by . . .

    1.

2.

3.

Rule Five: Remain task oriented.

We've broken this rule by . . .

We can apply this rule by . . .

1.

2.

3.

Rule Six: Allow for your partner to retreat with dignity.

We've broken this rule by . . .

We can apply this rule by . . .

1.

2.

3.

Rule Seven: Be proportional in your intensity.

We've broken this rule by . . .

We can apply this rule by . . .

1.

2.

3.

Conclusion:

A PERSONAL LETTER FROM ME TO YOU

You have come to the end of a book, but it's just the beginning of a different, better life than the one you've been living. I've written a book for you and your partner, and I sincerely hope that when you read it, it spoke to your hearts as well as your heads. I've done my part. Now it's your turn to take all that you've gained and make the most of it. It's time to win what you want. Take this opportunity to write a letter to yourself, right here and now. State boldly what you want. Assert the basis on which you deserve it. And claim the victory in a strong statement to yourself, to which you can return again and again. Then get out there and *live* it!

LETTER OF
INTENT

I, _____, am ready to . . .